ABOUT THE AUTHOR

Moustafa Gadalla was born in Cairo, Egypt in 1944. He graduated from Cairo University with a Bachelor of Science degree in civil engineering in 1967. He immigrated to the U.S.A. in 1971 to practice as a licensed professional engineer and land surveyor.

From his early childhood, Gadalla pursued his Ancient Egyptian roots with passion, through continuous study and research. Since 1990, he has dedicated and concentrated all his time to researching the Ancient Egyptian civilization. As an independent Egyptologist, he spends a part of every year visiting and studying sites of antiquities.

Gadalla is the author of nine internationally acclaimed books. He is the chairman of the Tehuti Research Foundation—an international, U.S.-based, non-profit organization, dedicated to Ancient Egyptian studies.

OTHER BOOKS BY THE AUTHOR

[See details on pages 237-240]

Egyptian Cosmology: The Animated Universe - 2nd ed.

Egyptian Divinities: The All Who Are THE ONE

Egyptian Harmony: The Visual Music

Historical Deception: The Untold Story of Ancient Egypt - 2nd ed.

Exiled Egyptians: The Heart of Africa

Pyramid Handbook - 2nd ed.

Tut-Ankh-Amen: The Livi

Egypt: A Pract

Egyptian Sufism: The

This Book is Dedicated to

The Baladi Egyptian Musicians,
The Most Humble and
The Most Talented

Book Production by: Moustafa Gadalla and Faith Cross
Book Cover Artwork by: K&D Design, North East, PA, USA

Egyptian Rhythm

The Heavenly Melodies

Moustafa Gadalla
Maa Kheru (True of Voice)

Tehuti Research Foundation
International Head Office: Greensboro, NC, U.S.A.

Egyptian Rhythm
The Heavenly Melodies
by Moustafa Gadalla

Published by:

Tehuti Research Foundation
P.O. Box 39406
Greensboro, NC 27438-9406, U.S.A.

Publisher's Cataloging in Publication Data
(Provided by Quality Books, Inc.)

Gadalla, Moustafa, 1944-
Egyptian rhythm : the heavenly melodies / Moustafa Gadalla. -- 1st ed.
p. cm.
Includes bibliographical references and index.
Library of Congress Control Number: 2002090118
ISBN: 1-931446-02-4

1. Music--Philosophy and aesthetics. 2. Music--Egypt--History and criticism. 3. Aesthetics, Egyptian. 4. Egypt--Antiques. I. Title.

ML3845.G33 2002 781.1'7'0932
QBI02-200125

Manufactured in the United States of America
Published 2002

Table of Contents

III Musical Formulations

IIII Musical Instruments

III Maintaining the Heavenly Rhythms

Appendices

Preface

Music and dance, nowadays, are considered to be types of "art". The term, "art", made it possible for anyone to qualify any absurdity and label it as a "work of art". The downhill trend in music started with Western academicians themselves, when in the 19th century they rejected the natural sounds of the harmonic and well balanced tones, in order to simplify the arithmetic explanation of music. They called their scheme, *scale temperament*. This tampering of music created unnatural tones, with different vibrational frequencies than those of the well balanced natural tones. [See Appendix A for more details.]

Western academia is quick to inform us that "intelligence" must overrule our sense of hearing. Consequently, they invoked new courses in "music appreciation", to force people to listen to their twisted "mathematics", not to the sound of music.

It should be noted that the keyboards of Mozart, Beethoven, and Bach were not tuned to the frequencies that are used in Western music today. These composers' works have been ruined by a combination of the use of unnatural tones, large ensembles, and the overpowering "new" musical instruments.

This book is intended to restore the musical faculties by uncovering the musical knowledge of Ancient Egypt. Musical life in Ancient Egypt has been ignored and denied by practically all Western musicologists. They are, in essence, denying themselves and the world of the most incredible source of music. We must note, however, the few Western musicologists who overcame Western and Judeao-Christian paradigms, to show the real accomplishments of Ancient Egypt. Among these few are the works of two distinguished Frenchmen: J. P. Roussier (1770) and F. J. Fétis (1837).

For the Ancient (and present-day Sufi) Egyptians, music was/is a mandatory subject for the education of youth; for to teach music, you teach everything. Plato acknowledged and endorsed the Ancient Egyptian musical system. He established the Ideal Laws in his ideal *Republic*, based solely and exclusively on the Ancient Egyptian system—as referred to throughout the book.

For the Ancient and *Baladi* (the present silent majority) Egyptians, music and dance are not abstract arts. For them, music is not just a way of life, it is life itself. It is as natural, critical, and vital as breathing.

Since all aspects of the universe are harmoniously interrelated, Egyptians can never separate music and dance from astronomy, geometry, mathematics, physics, theology, medicine, traditions, ...etc. The Egyptian musical system is a beautiful blend of all aspects of nature. Let the Egyptian Rhythm immerse you in the Heavenly Melodies. It is so beautiful. It is so intoxicating.

Moustafa Gadalla
To-beh 1, 13,000 (Ancient Egyptian Calendar)
January 9, 2002 CE

Standards and Terminology

1. Throughout this book, octave ranges are named according to the following system:

$$C_3 \quad C_2 \quad C_1 \quad C \quad c^1 \quad c^2 \quad c^3$$

<--- Lower Octaves --<---|--->-- Higher Octaves--->

2. Capital letters (*C, D, E,* etc) are reserved for general pitch names without regard to a specific octave range.

3. You may find a variety in writing the same Ancient Egyptian term, such as **Amen/Amon/Amun**. The reason is, that the vowels you see in translated Egyptian texts are approximations of sounds, which are used by Egyptologists to help them pronounce the Ancient Egyptian terms/words.

4. The Ancient Egyptian word, **neter**, and its feminine form **netert**, have been wrongly, and possibly intentionally, translated to *god* and *goddess*, by almost all academicians.

   Neteru (plural of **neter/netert**) are the divine principles and functions of the One Supreme God.

5. When referring to the names of cities, Pharaohs, **neteru**, etc., if the commonly used Greek name is different than the true Egyptian name, we will show the correct Egyptian name (**in this font**), followed by the "common" but arbitrary, Greek rendering between parentheses.

6. The term *Baladi* will be used throughout this book to denote the present silent majority of Egyptians that adhere to the Ancient Egyptian traditions, with a thin exterior layer of Islam. The Christian population of Egypt is an ethnic minority that came as refugees, from Judaea and Syria to the Ptolemaic/Roman-ruled Alexandria. Now, 2,000 years later, they are easily distinguishable in looks and mannerisms from the majority of native Egyptians. [See *Exiled Egyptians: The Heart of Africa*, by same author, and our website (http://www.egypt-tehuti.org), for detailed information.]

7. Throughout this book, the fonting of quotations varies depending on the source of quotation. There are generally two types of fonting:

   This font is used to refer to Ancient Egyptian sources.

   This font is used to refer to quotes from other sources.

Chronology of Egyptian Dynasties

Neolithic Period	before 5000 BCE
Pre-dynastic Period	c. 5000-3300 BCE
Protodynastic Period	c. 3300-3050 BCE

Dynasty	**Dates**	
I	3050 BCE - 2890 BCE	Early Dynastic Period
II	2890 BCE - 2649 BCE	
III	2649 BCE - 2575 BCE	
IV	2575 BCE - 2465 BCE	Old Kingdom
V	2465 BCE - 2323 BCE	
VI	2323 BCE - 2150 BCE	
VII-X - 1st Interm. Per.	2150 BCE - 2040 BCE	
XI	2040 BCE - 1991 BCE	Middle Kingdom
XII	1991 BCE - 1783 BCE	
XIII-XVII - 2nd Inter. Per.	1783 BCE - 1550 BCE	
XVIII	1550 BCE - 1307 BCE	New Kingdom
XIX	1307 BCE - 1196 BCE	
XX	1196 BCE - 1070 BCE	
XXI	1070 BCE - 712 BCE	3rd Intermed. Period
XXII	945 BCE - 712 BCE	
XXIII	878 BCE - 712 BCE	
XXIV	740 BCE - 712 BCE	
XXV	712 BCE - 657 BCE	Late Kingdom
XXVI	664 BCE - 525 BCE	
XXVII (Persian)	525 BCE - 404 BCE	
XXVIII	404 BCE - 399 BCE	
XXIX	399 BCE - 380 BCE	
XXX	380 BCE - 343 BCE	
Second Persian Period	343 BCE - 332 BCE	
Macedonian Kings	332 BCE - 304 BCE	Greco-Roman Period
Ptolemaic Dynasty	323 BCE - 30 BCE	
Roman Emperors	30 BCE - 323 CE	
Byzantine Emperors	323 CE - 642 CE	

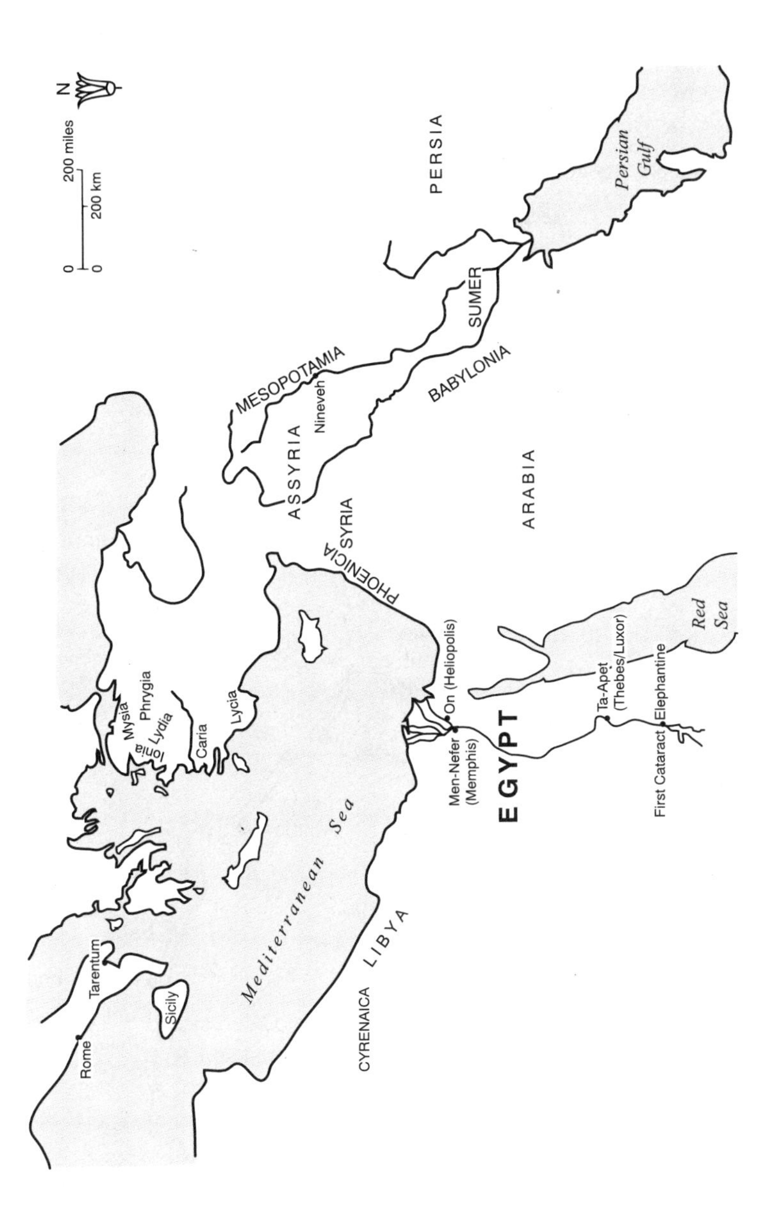

Map of Ancient Egypt and Surrounding Countries

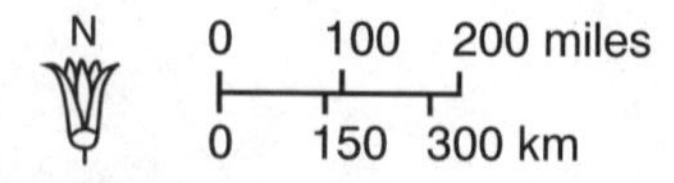
N
0 100 200 miles
0 150 300 km

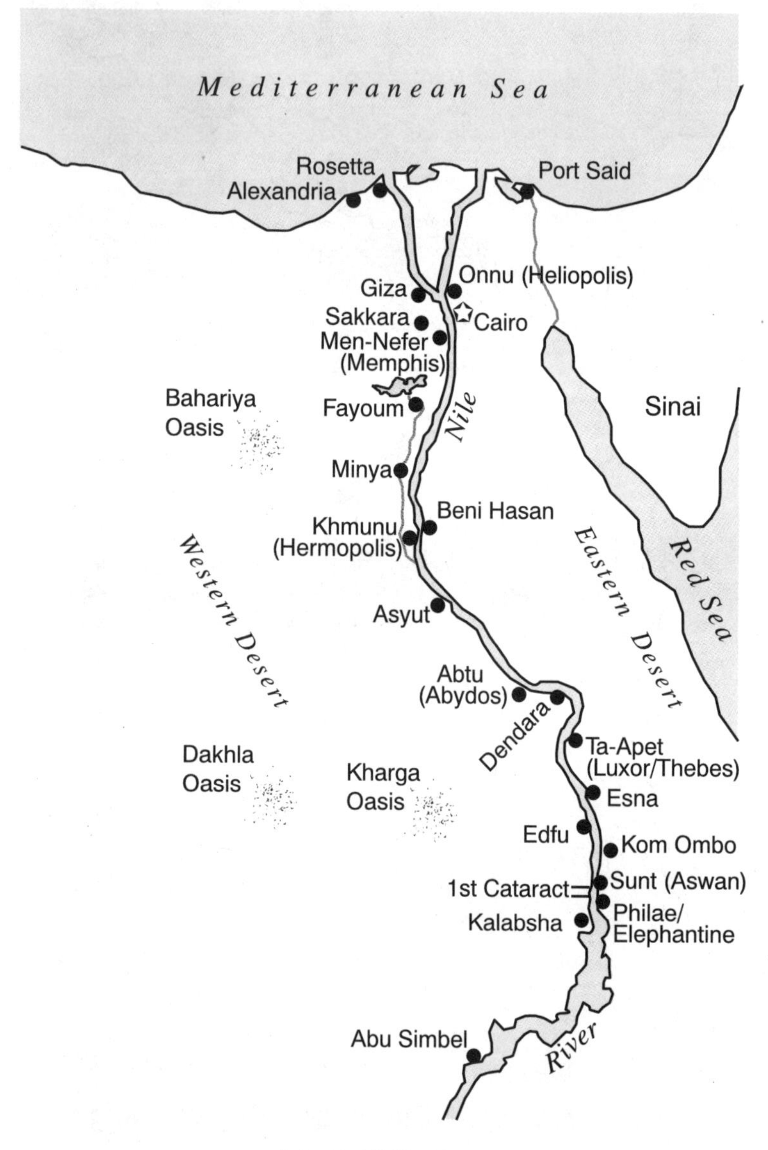
Mediterranean Sea
Rosetta
Alexandria
Port Said
Giza
Onnu (Heliopolis)
Sakkara
Cairo
Men-Nefer
(Memphis)
Bahariya
Oasis
Fayoum
Nile
Sinai
Minya
Beni Hasan
Khmunu
(Hermopolis)
Western Desert
Eastern Desert
Red Sea
Asyut
Abtu
(Abydos)
Dendara
Ta-Apet
(Luxor/Thebes)
Dakhla
Oasis
Kharga
Oasis
Esna
Edfu
Kom Ombo
1st Cataract
Sunt (Aswan)
Kalabsha
Philae/
Elephantine
Abu Simbel
River

Map of Egypt

Part

I

The Harmony of the Spheres

1

Cosmic Consciousness

Eye on the Sky

Herodotus, the Greek historian (500 BCE), stated:

Of all the nations of the world, the Egyptians are the happiest, healthiest and most religious.

The excellent condition of the Egyptians was attributed to their application of metaphysical realities in their daily life—in other words—total cosmic consciousness.

Egypt, recognizing the influence of the heavens on earth, observed the skies with the utmost attention. The data of astronomy was studied for its meaning, that is to say, the study of correspondences between events in the heavens and events on earth. Astronomy and astrology were, for them, two sides of the same coin.

A systematic kind of astronomical observation began in very early times. The most ancient astronomical texts, presently known, are found on the lids of wooden coffins dating from the 9th Dynasty (ca. 2150 BCE). These texts are called *diagonal calendars* or *diagonal star clocks*. They give the names of the decans (stars that rise at ten-day intervals at the same time as the sun), of which there are 36.

More elaborate star charts were found on the ceilings of numerous tombs from the New Kingdom (1550-1070 BCE).

While Western academia attributes the knowledge of astronomy to the Greeks, early historians reported otherwise. The great Strabo (64 BCE - 25 CE) admitted that:

> *The Egyptian priests are supreme in the science of the sky...[the Egyptians]...impart some of their precepts; although they conceal the greater part. [The Egyptians] revealed to the Greeks the secrets of the full year, whom the latter ignored as with many other things...*

"Modern" astronomy is attributed to the works of Johannes Kepler (1571-1630 CE), and he is credited with having "discovered" the three planetary laws. Yet none of these Western academicians tell us how Kepler arrived (out of thin air) at these conclusions. In truth, Kepler boasted in print, at the end of *Book V* of his series, *Harmony of the World*, that he rediscovered the lost laws of Egypt, as stated below:

> *Now, eighteen months after the first light, three months after the true day, but a very few days after the pure Sun of that most wonderful study began to shine, nothing restrains me; it is my pleasure to yield to the inspired frenzy, it is my pleasure to taunt mortal men with the candid acknowledgment that I am stealing the golden vessels of the Egyptians to build a tabernacle to my God from them, far, far away from the boundaries of Egypt.*

The jubilant Kepler did not state that he himself discovered anything. Rather, it was all Ancient Egyptian.

Harmony of the Spheres

The cosmic conscious Egyptians developed their music from the cosmos itself—the harmony of the spheres.

The Egyptian understanding of *universal harmony,* in an astronomical-musical sense, was confirmed by early Greek and Roman travelers. Diodorus of Sicily, in his *Book I* [Section 16-1], states:

> *It was by Tehuti [Thoth], according to ancient Egyptians. . . [who] was the first to observe the orderly arrangement of the stars and the harmony of the musical sounds and their nature.*

The intimate relationship between astronomy and music is the most important fundamental in the Egyptian thinking. This intimacy is manifested in all aspects of the Egyptian system—as we will see throughout this book.

Several Ancient Egyptian divinities (gods/goddesses) were associated with music. One of the main musical **neteru** (gods/goddesses) was **Het-Heru** (Hathor). Her shrines are spread throughout Egypt.

Het-Heru (Hathor) was/is called *The Seven* **Het-Heru**. Present-day *Baladi* Egyptians call her *Saba-banat* (meaning *Seven Maidens*).

Het-Heru represents the matrix of the metaphysical spiritual principle. Her association with the number 7—in this context—is consistent with the Ancient and *Baladi* Egyptian belief that the universal energy matrix consists of nine realms, which are commonly classified as *seven heavens* (metaphysical realms) and *two lands/earths* (physical realms).

The text of the beautiful *Hymn of the Seven* **Het-Heru**, in the Temple of Dendera, shows the intimate relationship between music and the cosmos:

> ***The sky and its stars make music to you.***
> ***The sun and the moon praise you.***
> ***The neteru exalt you.***
> ***The neteru sing to you.***

The text of this hymn consists of seven stanzas (equal to the seven metaphysical spheres). Each stanza consists of four lines (equal to a tetrachord).

Het-Heru (Hathor) is one of the Ancient Egyptians' very ancient divinities. The texts inscribed in the crypts of the temple of **Het-Heru** at Dendera clearly state that the temple (restored during the Ptolemaic Era) was based on drawings dating back to King Pepi of the 6th Dynasty (2400 BCE). The drawings themselves are copies of pre-dynastic documents. The text reads:

> ***The venerable foundation in Dendera was found in early writings, written on a leather roll in the time of the Servants of Heru*** *[the kings preceding Mena/Menes]*, ***at Men-Nefer*** *[Memphis]*, ***in a casket, at the time of the lord of the Two Lands... Pepi.'***

Het-Heru (Hathor) was called the *Mistress of Singing*, and the *Mistress of Dancing*. The seven **Het-Heru** represent the intimacy of music and dancing, to the seven planets nearest to us—on earth.

All swiftly vibrating, whirling (dancing) bodies produce sounds—like a vibrating string that produces sound when it is struck. The sound produced from the string depends—among other things—on its thickness/weight, the speed of its movement, and its distance from the human ear.

Likewise, the sounds (relative pitches) produced from the whirling planets are a function of the weights of the bodies, their particular speeds, and their relative position.

To recognize the impact on Earth by the heavenly sounds, Earth is considered unmoving at the center of all things. The seven planets that have impact on us Earth dwellers are, from the nearest to the farthest: Moon, Mercury, Venus, Sun, Mars, Jupiter, and Saturn. They revolve, some in a larger and some in a lesser orbit. Those that have the lesser orbit revolve faster, and those that have the larger revolve more slowly.

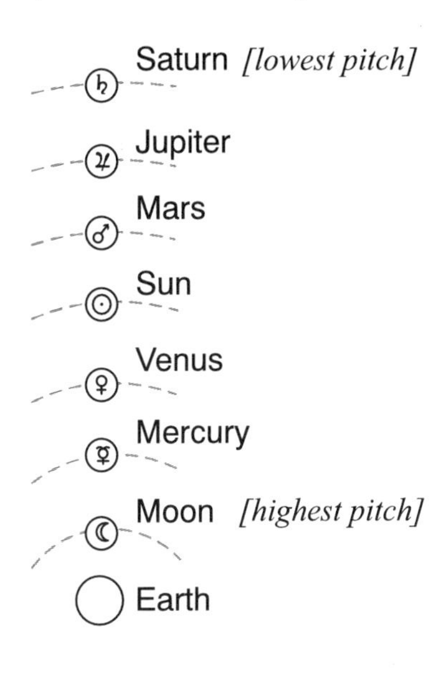

The Moon, situated nearest to the earth, is the swiftest-moving body, therefore producing a note of the highest pitch. Saturn, the highest in the heavens (and farthest from Earth), produces the lowest pitch.

The movement of the seven planets is melodious. The changing speed, direction, orbit distance, and sizes of the seven planets produce the seven natural tones known as the diatonic scale (*Do, Re, Mi, Fa, Sol, La, Si*).

The natural tones of the seven planets provided the archetype for both the Ancient Egyptian music and the days of the week. The Ancient Egyptians were the first to adopt the seven-day week as a consequence of the harmony of the seven spheres—as stated by Dio Cassius in his volumes, *Roman History* [Book XXXVII], as shown next.

2

Music All the Time (24 hours, 7 days)

The Ancient Egyptian application of the relationship between the seven days of the week, the natural tones of the diatonic scale, and the seven planets were clearly expressed by Dio Cassius (2nd century CE) in his volumes *Roman History, Book XXXVII* [Sections 18, 19], which stated unequivocally:

> ***The custom of referring the days to the seven stars called planets was instituted by the Egyptians****, but is now found among all mankind, though its adoption by other countries has been comparatively recent; at any rate the ancient Greeks never understood it. But since it is now quite the fashion with mankind generally and even with the Romans themselves, and for the Egyptians is already an ancestral tradition, I wish to write briefly of it, telling how and in what way it has been so arranged. I have heard two explanations, which are not difficult of comprehension, it is true, though they involve certain theories. For if you apply the* ***"principle of the tetrachord" (which is believed to constitute the basis of music) to these stars****, by which the whole universe of heaven is divided into regular intervals, in the order in which each of them revolves, and be-*

ginning at the outer orbit assigned to Saturn, then omitting the next two name the lord of the fourth, and after this passing over two others reach the seventh, and you then go back and repeat the process with the orbits and their presiding divinities in this same manner, assigning them to the several days, you will find ***all the days to be in a kind of musical connection with the arrangement of the heavens****. This is one of the explanations given; the other is as follows. If you begin at the first hour to count the hours of the day and of the night, assigning the first to Saturn, the next to Jupiter, the third to Mars, the fourth to the Sun, the fifth to Venus, the sixth to Mercury, and the seventh to the Moon, according to the order of the cycles which the Egyptians observe, and if you repeat the process, covering thus the whole 24 hours, you will find that the first hour of the following day comes to the Sun. And if you carry on the operation throughout the next 24 hours in the same manner as with the others, you will dedicate the first hour of the third day to the Moon, and if you proceed similarly through the rest, each day will receive its appropriate planet. This, then, is the [Egyptian] tradition.*

See the 24x7 Ancient Egyptian musical pattern, as per the above statement of Dio Cassius, on pages 26 and 27.

Dio Cassius' statement attests to these main facts:

1. The relationship between the seven days of the week and the harmonic natural sounds of the diatonic scale was instituted by the Ancient Egyptians. Such a relationship was a consequence of the heavenly music of the seven (wandering) planets.

> *The custom of referring the days to the seven stars called planets was instituted by the Egyptians. . .*
> *. . .and to them already an ancestral tradition. . .*

2. The relationship between the seven planets and the days

Hours of the Day

Day		1	2	3	4	5	6	7	8	9	10	11
♄ Saturday		♄ 1 *si*	♃ 2 *do*	♂ 3 *re*	☉ 4 *mi*	♀ 5 *fa*	☿ 6 *sol*	☾ 7 *la*	♄ 1 *si*	♃ 2 *do*	♂ 3 *re*	☉ 4 *mi*
☉ Sunday	Tetrachord	☉ 4 *mi*	♀ 5 *fa*	☿ 6 *sol*	☾ 7 *la*	♄ 1 *si*	♃ 2 *do*	♂ etc.. *re*	☉ *mi*	♀ *fa*	☿ *sol*	☾ *la*
☾ Monday	Tetrachord	☾ *la*	♄ *si*	♃ *do*	♂ *re*	☉ *mi*	♀ *fa*	☿ *sol*	☾ *la*	♄ *si*	♃ *do*	♂ *re*
♂ Tuesday	Tetrachord	♂ *re*	☉ *mi*	♀ *fa*	☿ *sol*	☾ *la*	♄ *si*	♃ *do*	♂ *re*	☉ *mi*	♀ *fa*	☿ *sol*
☿ Wednesday	Tetrachord	☿ *sol*	☾ *la*	♄ *si*	♃ *do*	♂ *re*	☉ *mi*	♀ *fa*	☿ *sol*	☾ *la*	♄ *si*	♃ *do*
♃ Thursday	Tetrachord	♃ *do*	♂ *re*	☉ *mi*	♀ *fa*	☿ *sol*	☾ *la*	♄ *si*	♃ *do*	♂ *re*	☉ *mi*	♀ *fa*
♀ Friday	Tetrachord	♀ *fa*	☿ *sol*	☾ *la*	♄ *si*	♃ *do*	♂ *re*	☉ *mi*	♀ *fa*	☿ *sol*	☾ *la*	♄ *si*

Hours of the Night

12	1	2	3	4	5	6	7	8	9	10	11	12
♀ 5 ***fa***	☿ 6 ***sol***	☾ 7 ***la***	♄ 1 ***si***	♃ 2 ***do***	♂ 3 ***re***	☉ 4 ***mi***	♀ 5 ***fa***	☿ 6 ***sol***	☾ 7 ***la***	♄ 1 ***si***	♃ 2 ***do***	♂ 3 ***re***
♄ ***si***	♃ ***do***	♂ ***re***	☉ ***mi***	♀ ***fa***	☿ ***sol***	☾ ***la***	♄ ***si***	♃ ***do***	♂ ***re***	☉ ***mi***	♀ ***fa***	☿ ***sol***
☉ ***mi***	♀ ***fa***	☿ ***sol***	☾ ***la***	♄ ***si***	♃ ***do***	♂ ***re***	☉ ***mi***	♀ ***fa***	☿ ***sol***	☾ ***la***	♄ ***si***	♃ ***do***
☾ ***la***	♄ ***si***	♃ ***do***	♂ ***re***	☉ ***mi***	♀ ***fa***	☿ ***sol***	☾ ***la***	♄ ***si***	♃ ***do***	♂ ***re***	☉ ***mi***	♀ ***fa***
♂ ***re***	☉ ***mi***	♀ ***fa***	☿ ***sol***	☾ ***la***	♄ ***si***	♃ ***do***	♂ ***re***	☉ ***mi***	♀ ***fa***	☿ ***sol***	☾ ***la***	♄ ***si***
☿ ***sol***	☾ ***la***	♄ ***si***	♃ ***do***	♂ ***re***	☉ ***mi***	♀ ***fa***	☿ ***sol***	☾ ***la***	♄ ***si***	♃ ***do***	♂ ***re***	☉ ***mi***
♃ ***do***	♂ ***re***	☉ ***mi***	♀ ***fa***	☿ ***sol***	☾ ***la***	♄ ***si***	♃ ***do***	♂ ***re***	☉ ***mi***	♀ ***fa***	☿ ***sol***	☾ ***la***

of the week (as practiced by the Egyptians), according to Dio Cassius, started with Saturn.

> *Beginning at the outer orbit assigned to Saturn ... all the days to be in a kind of musical connection with the arrangement of heavens...*

3. The principles of the tetrachords were implemented in the Ancient Egyptian musical system, to the above mentioned sequence of the seven planets. Dio Cassius stated,

> *If you apply the "principle of the tetrachord" (which is believed to constitute the basis of music) to these stars, . . .*

Tetrachord is a word that simply means four strings. The essential parts of the tetrachord were/are the top and bottom strings. These made a Perfect Fourth with each other. The "Perfect Fourth", as such, is the sound made by the fourth natural tone from any given note. If we start the scale at, say *C* (*Do*), its fourth will be *F* (*Fa*) in the ascending scale.

The Ancient Egyptian Musical Master Plan [pgs 26-27] shows how the days of the week form a Perfect Fourth between them. Examples:

Sunday–Monday: ***Mi***, *Fa, Sol*, ***La*** (**E**, F, G, **A**)

Thursday–Friday: ***Do***, *Re, Mi*, ***Fa*** (**C**, D, E, **F**)

4. The division of the day into 24 hours also comes from the Egyptians.
By applying the first of the planets (Saturn) to the first hour of the first day of the week, and in each following hour, the next planet, in the order stated previously,

we will find, by repeating alternatively the same order, that the first hour of the second day will correspond to the *Sun*; the first of the third, to the *Moon,* and so on. [See Master Plan on pgs 26-27.]

The division of the day into 24 hours and the week into 7 days provides the perfect harmonious pattern, where the order of hours (days) coincides with the distribution by Fourths between consecutive days. In other words, one system could not be established without the other.

5. Dio Cassius stated specifically that neither the Greeks nor the Romans have divided the day into hours, nor the month into portions of seven days, or weeks. It is from the Egyptians, as Dio Cassius testifies, that the other peoples have taken this usage.

> *. . .its adoption by other countries has been comparatively recent; at any rate the ancient Greeks never understood it. But since it is now quite the fashion with mankind generally and even with the Romans themselves,* ***and for the Egyptians is already an ancestral tradition****.*

6. The purely Egyptian 24x7 musical table provides a system with coordinate axes that correspond with the Ancient Egyptian game of checkers, which was the basis for choosing proper tones and modes—based on the diagonals drawn from a particular reference point. This type of thinking concurs with the Egyptian astronomical texts that are called *diagonal calendars* and *diagonal star clocks*. In other words, the choice of proper tones and modes is intimately related to the harmony of the spheres.

3

Energizing the Diatonic Week

The Natural Musical Scale

Before we proceed with more information about the Ancient Egyptian knowledge, we should review some simple terms and fundamentals—in our modern-day nomenclature.

- Consider a string of a given length as unity. Set it vibrating; it produces a sound—shown here as *Do*.
- Stop the string at its midpoint and set half of it vibrating. The frequency of vibrations produced is double that given by the whole string, and the tone is raised by one octave [shown herein as *Do*^{1}].
- Between the original note (produced from the whole length—*Do*) and the sound produced at the halfpoint—its octave—*Do*^{1}, there are six positions where the ear interprets six different harmonious sounds (*Re, Mi, Fa, Sol, La, Si*), located at unequal distances from each other. The reaction to all the sounds of natural tones is characterized by an unmistakable sense of equilibrium.

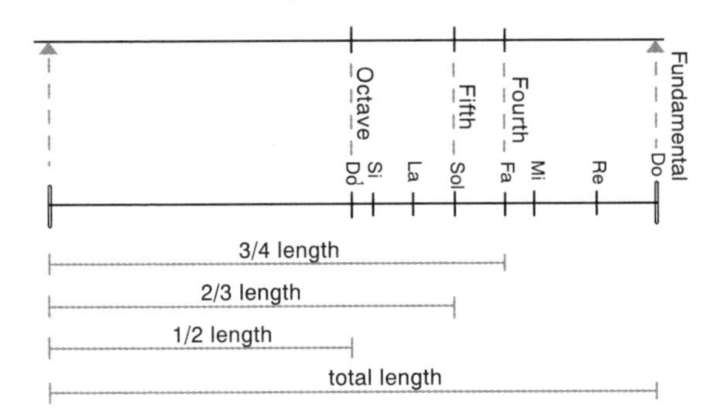

- The seven natural sounds are given the letters *A, B, C, D, E, F,* and *G*, for the syllables: *La, Si, Do, Re, Mi, Fa,* and *Sol*.
  The interval between each of these tones is as follows (using *Do* (*C*) as a starting point):

Do and *Re*	(*C* and *D*)	whole tone
Re and *Mi*	(*D* and *E*)	whole tone
Mi and *Fa*	(*E* and *F*)	semitone
Fa and *Sol*	(*F* and *G*)	whole tone
Sol and *La*	(*G* and *A*)	whole tone
La and *Si*	(*A* and *B*)	whole tone
Si and *Do*	(*B* and C^1)	semitone

The distinction between a whole tone and semitone can easily be recognized on a keyboard. The interval between *Do* (*C*) and *Re* (*D*) has a black key between them and is therefore that of a *whole tone*, but between *Mi* (*E*) and *Fa* (*F*) and *Si* (*B*) and *Do* (*C*) where the black key is missing, the interval is only that of a semitone.

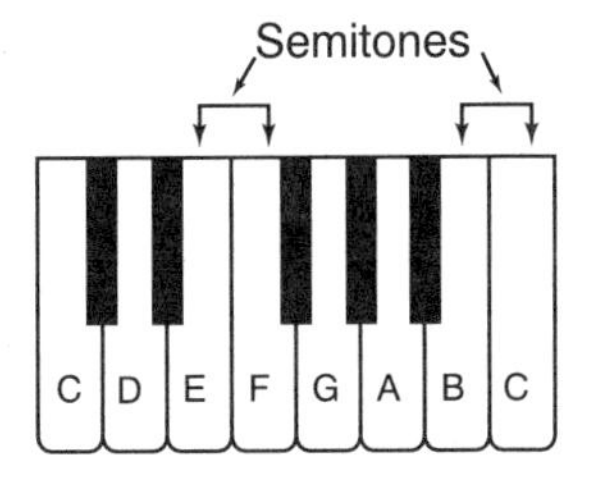

As such, each diatonic scale has two semitones—between *E* (*Mi*) and *F* (*Fa*) and *B* (*Si*) and *C* (*Do*).

The diatonic scale (*A, B, C, D, E, F, G*) can begin from any natural sound, say *C*, until it reaches its octave at C^1 (in a rising series—ascending), or to C_1 (in a lowering series—descending).

Therefore, there are seven types of diatonic scales, in each direction—up and down. Each scale is referred to by its first tone, such as C-scale, D-scale, etc. Some examples are shown below.

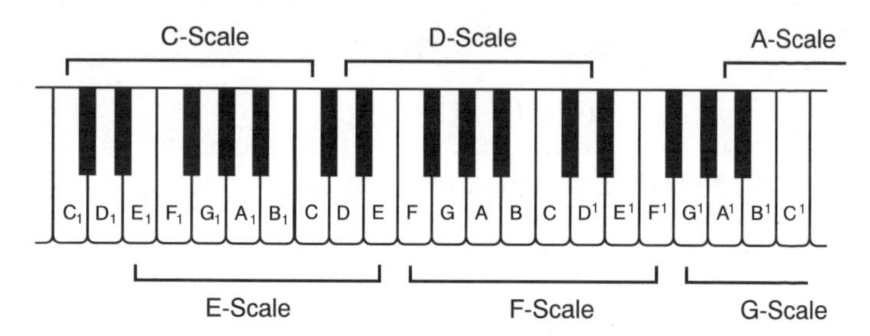

The Two Energy Centers

The present silent majority of the Egyptian people (*Baladi*) correlate specific activities of their daily life to certain days of the week. These activities are concentrated in two focal periods: the Eve of Monday (Sunday night) and the Eve of Friday (Thursday night), with more focus on the Eve of Friday (this has absolutely nothing to do with Islam, whatsoever). Marriage ceremonies are only allowed on these two nights, with preference to Friday Eve. Thousands of local shrines (nothing related to Islam) are visited on both these eves, with special preference to Friday Eve. People spend the night of Friday Eve at the tombs of their departed relatives (contrary to Islam). Intercourse between married couples is very special on Friday Eve. Courtship activities of all kinds are more prevalent on Friday Eve. All types of activities (cutting hair, butcher work, ...etc) follow the same pattern.

Since Ancient Egyptian times, the week started on a high (musical) note, namely Saturday. [Equating Saturday to Saturn, the highest, will be clarified at the end of this chapter.] As such, the layout of the week, with the two special focal eves will look as follows:

Saturday

Sunday
Monday } Lightly Active

Tuesday

Wednesday

Thursday
Friday } Very Active

Saturday

The concentrated activities towards both ends of the week (with two centers of activity—one more prominent than the other) correspond to an elliptical form that conforms to Kepler's first planetary law.

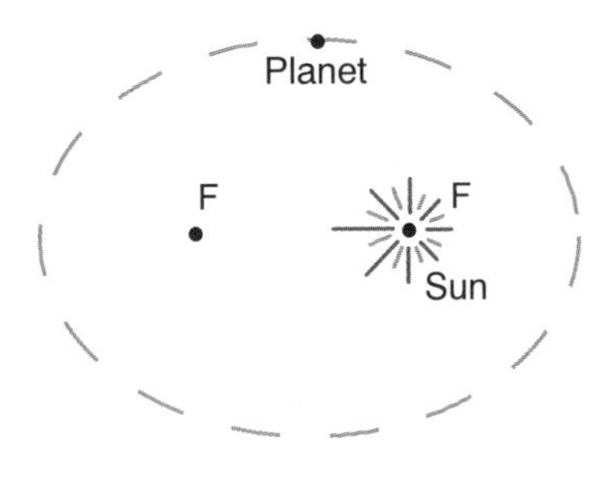

Johannes Kepler (1571-1630) rediscovered—from Egyptian sources—that the orbit of a planet/comet about its sun is an egg-shaped path (ellipse). Each planetary system is balanced only when the planet's orbit is an egg-shaped plane that has two foci, with its sun's center of mass at one of its foci. Similarly, the Egyptian traditions follow the same pattern. All aspects of their thinking and society can be reasoned to the egg-shaped characteristics—including music.

The Egyptian Dorian Scale

The most popular sequence of the diatonic scale throughout the Egyptian history (ancient and present) is the brightest scale, namely the D-scale, which goes:

D—E•F—G—A—B•C—D^1
[—denotes full interval, • denotes half interval]

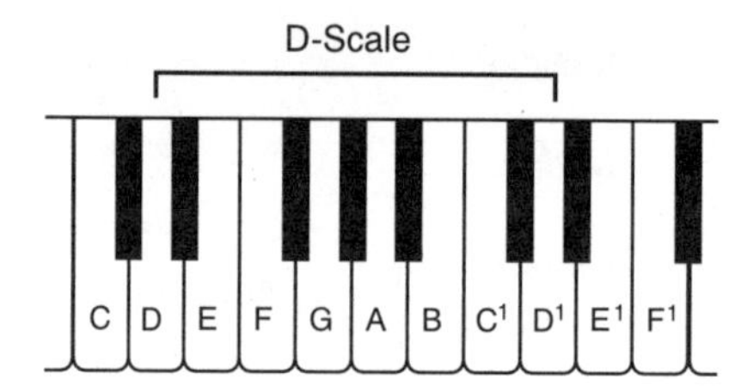

Because of the presence of two half-intervals in the diatonic scale between *E–F* and *B–C*, the D-scale is the only symmetrical scale in both directions—either ascending or descending.

By applying the sequence of the seven natural sounds of the D-scale to the seven days of the week, we get:

Saturday	D [Re]	
Sunday Monday	E [Mi] F [Fa]	} Semitone
Tuesday	G [Sol]	
Wednesday	A [La]	
Thursday Friday	B [Si] C [Do]	} Semitone
Saturday	D^1 $[Re]^1$	

One cannot help but notice the symmetry of the weekdays that is also shaped like an ellipse with two focal points at Sunday–Monday and Thursday–Friday. This scale is identical to the Egyptians' traditions of weekly polar activities, as stated earlier.

The ascending D-scale is the model for one's deliberate communications with higher realms. In an ascending D-scale, the first 'interval' (semitone) comes between *E* (*Mi*) and *F* (*Fa*). Not too much energy is required at this juncture, and the octave develops smoothly to *B* (*Si*). However, the second semitone between *B* (*Si*) and *C* (*Do*) needs much stronger energy for its required development than between *E* (*Mi*) and *F* (*Fa*), because the vibrations of the octave at this point are of a considerably higher pitch. These are the reasons for the light Egyptian activities at Sunday–Monday and the greater activities at Thursday–Friday.

The descending D-scale represents the communications between the higher realms and our earthly realm. Taken in the downward direction, a descending octave develops much more easily than an ascending octave. Supernatural forces require less effort to communicate with us on earth. The first semitone occurs right away, between *C* (*Do*) and *B* (*Si*). Not much energy is required at this juncture, where the energy needed is often found either in the *C* (*Do*) itself or in the lateral vibrations evoked by *C* (*Do*). The octave develops smoothly to *F* (*Fa*). The second semitone *F–E* (*Fa-Mi*) requires a considerably less strong shock than the first.

The most favored scale in Egypt is called *Bayati*. It is a D-scale and thus provides the perfect harmonious communication between the above and the below—to and from.

The D-scale was known in ancient Greece as the *Dorian* scale/mode. We will find later that **Dor-ian** is an Egyptian term that was and continues to be used in Egypt.

Sabt, The Leader of the Band

We stated earlier that the first day of the week in Ancient (and present-day) Egypt is Saturday. The term, Saturday—in earlier Latin texts—was called Saturn-day, i.e. referring to Saturn. The planet Saturn was called *Sabeth/Sabbath,* according to early Latin writers such as Epiphane.

The term, Saturday, in Ancient (and present-day) Egypt is **Sabt**, which means (in Ancient Egyptian language) *Sirius*, also known as the Dog Star.

Plutarch, based on the Ancient Egyptian traditions *[Treatise of Isis & of Osiris]*, equated **Anbu** (Anubis) with Saturn. **Anbu**, symbolized by the dog, is called *Kyein* in the Greek language. For that reason, the Greeks referred to Saturn as Kronos *(Kyon),* which means *dog*.

Anbu represented the Divine Guide in Ancient Egypt. The dog symbolizes the divine guide because of its homing instinct day or night. The dog leads.

The Dog Star

The Ancient Egyptian calendar is based on the heliacal rising of **Sabt** (Sirius, The Dog Star). Music and the calendar are intimately related, as we will see throughout this book.

Sabt (Sirius—The Dog Star) is referred to as the First, and the D-scale is also referred to as the First scale. All generated music is a variation of this First scale.

In the harmony of the spheres, **Sabt**, the Dog Star, leads the Cosmic Musical Band.

Part

The Harmonic Laws

4

The Egyptian Roots of Harmonic Laws

Egypt's Ideal Laws & Plato

In order to achieve harmony within each of us—as well as among the society as a whole—our music and dance must concur with the cosmic harmonic laws.

An Ancient Egyptian playing the lyre

In Ancient Egypt, the impact of the double-edge powers of music, to both soothe and stir the mind, was recognized and reflected in their musical system. Likewise, Plato urged that the Ideal State be erected upon the foundation of music and that any change in the traditional ways of music be resisted, in order to protect the welfare of the State. Plato's recommendation was the adoption of Ancient Egypt's system and practices, as shown throughout the book.

Ancient Egypt was Plato's only source for his Ideal Laws, and the plan that he laid down for the education of youth follows precisely the plan that was developed long ago by the Egyptians.

> *ATHENIAN: Every means, then, shall* ***we say, must be employed to keep our children from the desire to reproduce different models in dance or song****, . .* ***can any of us find a better device for this purpose than that employed in Egypt? . . . [where] . . . the plan is to consecrate all our dances and all our tunes****.*
>
> *Plato [Laws VII, 798e–799b]*

Plato also admitted that musical "theory" did exist in Ancient Egypt, and was detailed by appropriate rules and laws.

> *Long ago the Egyptians determined on the rule ... that the youth of a State should practice in their rehearsals postures and tunes that are harmonically pleasing. These they prescribed in detail and posted up in the temples ... As regards music, it has proved possible for* ***the tunes, which possess a natural correctness to be enacted by law and permanently consecrated****.*
>
> *Plato [Laws, 656-7]*

The existence of a considerable number of Ancient Egyptian works were known and utilized by the Greeks. A few of the historical acknowledgements of the availability of the Egyptian works are presented herein:

1. Practically all notable Greeks went to Egypt for education, as noted by Diodorus of Sicily, *Book I* [96. 1-2]:

   *But now that we have examined these matters, we must enumerate what Greeks, who have won fame for their wisdom and learning, **visited Egypt in ancient times, in order to become acquainted with its customs and learning... Homer and Lycurgus of Sparta, and Plato,** and that there also came **Pythagoras of Samos and the mathematician Eudoxus** [The famous astronomer, geographer, and mathematician of Cnidus, pupil of Plato.]... [For instance, according to Strabo (17. 1. 29), in Heliopolis were pointed out the houses where Plato and Eudoxus had stopped.].*

2. Clement Alexandrinus (200 CE) mentions 42 volumes accredited to the Egyptian **Tehuti** (*Hermes* is its Greek rendering) on various subjects. **Two books were on music**, four others on astronomy, one containing a list of the fixed stars, another on the phenomena of the sun and moon, two others on the rising of the stars. Another contained a cosmography and geography, **the course of the sun, moon, and the five planets**. These volumes were part of the available written information in the Library of Alexandria, which contained hundreds of thousands of similar Ancient Egyptian documents—in their original Egyptian language and/or in their Greek translations—all written on Egyptian papyri.

3. The skill of the Egyptians, in the use of musical instruments, was also affirmed by Athenaeus, who stated (in his texts [iv, 25]) that both the Greeks and barbarians were taught music by Egyptian natives.

4. More about the Egyptian roots of Greek music, such as the Egyptian **Dor-ians**, is presented throughout this book.

The Egyptian Dor-ians

Plato, Aristotle, Plutarch, and other Greek notables were writing in their time about the poor status of music in their country. They always made reference to an older and more superior system of music in the Greek Isles. This older system was based on the **Dor-ian** musical system. Old Greek texts on music always use **Dor-ian** as an adjective: **Dor-ian** mode, **Dor-ian** scale, ...etc.

Herodotus (500 BCE), the Greek father of history, stated that he came from Halicarnassus, a **Dor-ian** town. He clearly stated the connection between the **Dor-ians** and Egypt, in *The Histories* [Book Six, Sections 53-55]:

[53] . . . if one were to trace back, generation by generation, the lineage of Danaë the daughter of Acrisius, the chiefs of the Dorians would turn out to be true-born Egyptians.

[55] Enough has been said about all this. Others have explained how and through what achievements they became kings over the Dorians, despite being Egyptians, and so I will not go into that. I will record things that others have not picked up.

Herodotus, in [55] above, stated that such a fact was common knowledge at his time (500 BCE) and needed no elaboration.

Other similarities between the **Dor-ians** and Egyptians were made reference to, several times by Herodotus, such as in *The Histories* [Book Two, Section 91].

The Egyptian **Dor-ian** influence extended throughout the Mediterranean basin. At Tarentum in southern Italy, the celebrated Pythagorean center was established by Pythagoras and his followers, after he spent 20 years study-

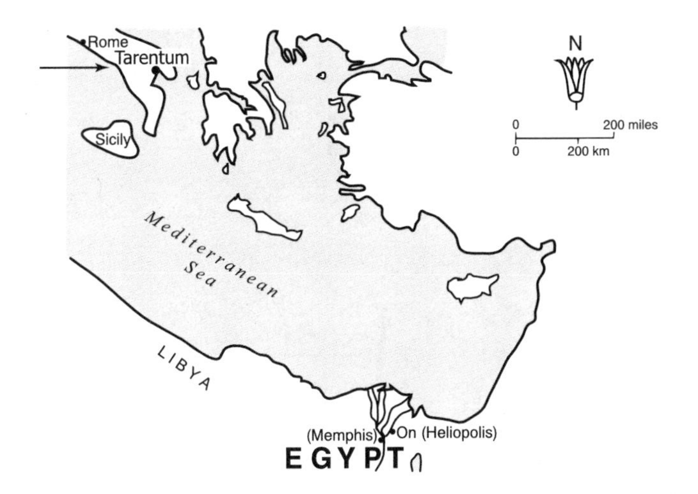

ing in Egypt, in the 5th century BCE. The center became their great cultural and philosophical headquarters. The Doric language of the **Dor-ians** was spoken in the Peloponnese, various Greek islands, and in Magna Graecia, in southern Italy, where Tarentum was established.

On the subject of music, this Doric/**Dor-ian** region in southern Italy provided notables such as:

- Philolaus, a known celebrated Pythagorean.
- Archytas of Tarentum (ca. 400 BCE).
- Aristoxenos of Tarentum (ca. 320 BCE).

Their writings show traces of the Ancient Egyptian system that was handed down to them by Pythagoras. But because of a loss of principle, their writings are fragmented, erroneous, and confusing. [See Appendix C for more information.]

Other aspects of the Egyptian **Dor-ians** will be stated throughout the book.

5

Ma-at,
The Law of Balance

To understand music (or any subject), the Egyptians always started at Ground Zero—the beginning point of creation. Whoever does not master the first principles will never master the subject.

For the deeply religious people of Egypt, the creation of the universe was not a physical event (Big Bang) that just happened. The explosion (Big Bang) that led to the creation of the universe was an orderly event—unlike all other explosions that exhibit a random and disordered form. **Ma-at** symbolizes the orderly Divine Law that governs the physical and metaphysical aspects of the world.

Ma-at is the **netert** (goddess) that represents the principle of cosmic order. The concept by which not only men, but also the **neteru** (gods) themselves were governed, and without which the **neteru** (gods) are functionless. **Ma-at** signifies harmony, balance and equilibrium—between all the different cosmic forces (**neteru**).

Harmony is characterized by an unmistakable sense of 'equilibrium'. Equilibrium is a state in which positive and negative forces are balanced. **Ma-at** is usually depicted next to a balanced scale.

The world as we know it is held together by a law that is based on the balanced dual nature of all things (wholes, units). Balance occurs between complementary opposites.

As stated earlier, planets are kept in balance by following an egg-shaped orbit with two foci that have unequal energy centers.

Ma-at is usually depicted next to the typical Ancient Egyptian scale—with two unequal weights—and therefore requiring balancing by the plumb bob. The plumb bob determines the vertical and governs the equilibrium of the scales. Scenes of weighing show that it is necessary to still the plumb line, because otherwise it would continue to oscillate. The Ancient Egyptian term for oscillation, intoxication, and plumb bob is **tkh**.

The plumb bob, **tkh**, is very often modeled in the form of the heart, **ib**, *the Dancer*. The heartbeat provides us with a convenient measure of time. [Also see page 91.]

Music is all about balance. Maintaining **Ma-at** is to maintain harmony, balance, and equilibrium in everything—including music. **Ma-at's** representations are found as "decoration" on many Egyptian instruments. The experts in music were called *musicians/priests of* **Ma-at** and teaching instruments were/are called *Mizan*—meaning balance/scale.

6

Tehuti, The Divine Sound

Orderly Sounds

As stated in the previous chapter, the sound explosion (Big Bang) that led to the creation of the world was an orderly event. The differentiation between the varied natures of sound, as well as the written forms (words, language) of sounds, was founded by the Egyptians—as stated in Plato *Collected Dialogues,* in *Philebus* [18-b,c,d]:

> *SOCRATES: The unlimited variety of sound was once discerned by some god, or perhaps some godlike man; you know the story that there was some such person in Egypt called Theuth.*
>
> *He it was who originally discerned the existence, in that unlimited variety, of:*
>
> - *the vowels—not 'vowel' in the singular but 'vowels' in the plural—and then of*
> - *other things which, though they could not be called articulate sounds, yet were noises of a kind. There*

were a number of them too, not just one, and

- *as a third class he discriminated what we now call the mutes.*

Having done that, he divided up the noiseless ones or mutes until he got each one by itself, and did the same thing with the vowels and the intermediate sounds; in the end he found a number of the things, and affixed to the whole collection, as to each single member of it, the name 'letter.'

It was because he realized that none of us could ever get to know one of the collection all by itself, in isolation from all the rest, that he conceived of 'letter' as a kind of bond of unity, uniting as it were all these sounds into one, and so he gave utterance to the expression 'art of letters,' implying that there was one art that dealt with the sounds.

The reference to *Theuth* above is the same *Theuth* mentioned in *Phaedrus*, where we are explicitly told that he was an Ancient Egyptian **neter** (god), *"the one whose sacred bird is called the Ibis"*, so as to exclude all doubt about his identity. It is obvious that his account is based on a genuine Egyptian tradition, because the ibis-headed **Tehuti** (Thoth) is an Egyptian **neter** (god).

Plato, in *Philebus* [18-b,c,d], tells us (in his obscure way) that:

1. The Egyptian **Tehuti** (Theuth/Thoth) was the first to observe the *infinity of sound*.

2. **Tehuti** (Thoth) divided up the infinity of sound into three distinct categories: *regular vibrations (pitch)*, *random vibrations (noise)*, and *the absence of sound (muting)*.

   Mutation is the separation/differentiation in time and space between the different tones. Without proper mutations, we have chaos. The proper separation of sounds enable us to distinguish and recognize each sound, and how the consecutive sounds relate to each other. In other words, mutation identifies the distance/time between two sounds—the *interval*.

   Mutations also set the different rhythmic patterns—the different tempos. [More information about rhythmic timing in chapter 12].

3. **Tehuti** (Thoth) set the principle of the written language—letters—as the graphic representation (image/picture) of the spoken/sound vibrations. In other words, the Ancient Egyptian written symbols (letters) are sound realities—visual music.

Language and/of Music

The last point above (#3) illustrates the intimate relationship between the sound and the visual aspects of the Ancient Egyptian language and/of music.

Each letter/sound has its own distinguishable vibrational pattern. To illustrate that letters are sonic pictures, below are some examples of the waveform for different sounds. On the left is *sh* as in *shoe*, in the middle is the vowel *ah*, and on the right is the diagram for "white" noise.

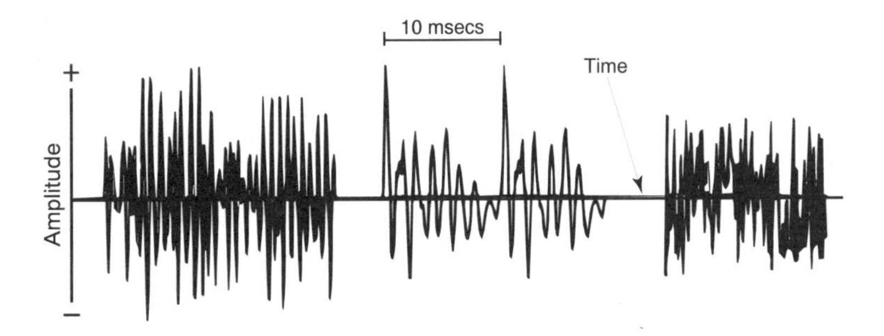

The composition of words and phrases in Ancient Egypt followed the same rules for musical composition. The Egyptian words were constructed of their symbols (letters), so that the meaning of a word emerged from the interplay of symbols—as the meaning of a chord or a musical phrase results from the combination of notes.

The Ancient Egyptian language allows it to be written in all directions—up, down, right, left. Music flows in the same pattern—ascending and descending, back and forth.

The structure of the Ancient Egyptian words followed the same principles of musical formulation. The fundamental musical law of reciprocity/inversion applies also to word structure. For example, the Ancient Egyptian words, **Neb** and **Ben** (**Neb** backwards) have opposite meanings. [Read more about this subject in *Egyptian Harmony: The Visual Music*, by same author.]

More information about the intimacy between music and language can be found in chapters 11 and 18.

Tehuti, the Master of Eight (Octave)

Tehuti (*Hermes* to the Greeks, *Mercury* to the Romans) was/is called *Master of the City of Eight.* This city was/is called **Khmunu** (*Hermopolis* by the Greeks), which means *Eight.* **Tehuti** represents the orderly flow of sounds. **Tehuti's** number—eight—is the rhythmic number in the universe.

As stated earlier, Ancient and *Baladi* Egyptians believe that the universal energy matrix consists of nine realms, which are commonly classified as *seven heavens* (metaphysical realms) and *two lands/earths* (physical realms).

The human race exists at number 8, the *first land/earth* [the ninth realm will be discussed on page 68]. The human being is said to be created in the image of God, the First Principle. Our earthly existence at the 8th realm is a replication and not a duplication—an octave.

Musically, the eighth natural tone of any given tone is the octave of such a natural tone. On the keyboard shown here, D^1 is the ascending octave of D. The octave, as such, represents the renewal theme of eight terms, because it reaches through all eight intervals of the scale.

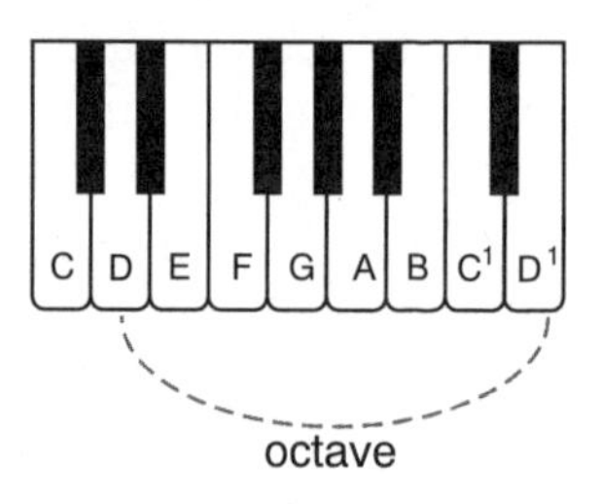

The eight term octave was called *Harmonia* or *harmonic octachord scale,* and was described in early Greek writings as the **Dor-ian** octachord—structured based on the Octave, Fourth, and Fifth—the three consonant intervals. These three consonant intervals relate to the three seasons of the Ancient Egyptian calendar, as we will see next.

7

The Musical Model

The Rhythms of the Three Seasons

Everything in the universe—large or small—has its own rhythm. Rhythm means flow: a movement that surges and recedes in intensity, and the water is the best physical representation of flow.

In their typical storyform fashion, the Ancient Egyptians described the major aspects of music, its laws, cosmic connections, etc., as it relates to the seasonal changes of the Nile River—and not climatic changes. The Egyptian symbols for each season and month were entirely water-related [see chart on page 53].

In his *Book I* [Section 16-1], Diodorus of Sicily states:

> *It was by Tehuti [Hermes for the Greeks], according to ancient Egyptians. . . [who]* ***was the first to observe the orderly arrangement*** *of the stars and the harmony of the musical sounds and their nature.*
> *He also made a lyre and gave it* ***three strings, imitating the seasons of the year; for he adopted three tones, a high, a low, and a medium****; [to correspond to the fluctuation of the River Nile flow].*

The *lyre*, mentioned in Diodorus' statement, is a Greek word that signifies *system* or *canon*, based on a string instrument. The Egyptian term, **Ka-Nun** (pronounced in Arabic as *ka-noon*), also signifies *rule/law*, not only in Egypt, but also in Latin languages, such as the English word, *canon*.

Examples of the symbolism in **Tehuti's** *lyre* (system), regarding the definition of harmonics, are:

1. A three-stringed instrument allows the playability in several ways:
   a. solo playing—one note at a time across the three strings;
   b. two tones together/simultaneously;
   c. the chordal playing of the simultaneous sounding of three pitches. That is to say, the assemblage of sounds that we call *harmony*.

2. **Tehuti's** three-stringed instrument provides/represents the most perfect form of organized scale, which unites the three innate intervals: Fourth, Fifth, and Octave. As stated earlier, the **Dor-ian** octachord was structured from these three musical intervals.

   The intervals of Fourth, Fifth, and Octave were the most common in Ancient Egyptian representations. [See page 112 for related studies and conclusions.]

- As mentioned earlier, the Fourth is the sound made by the fourth natural tone from any given note. If we start the scale at, say *C* (*Do*), its Fourth will be *F* (*C, D, E,* ***F***) in ascending scale.

- The Fifth is the sound made by the fifth natural tone from any given

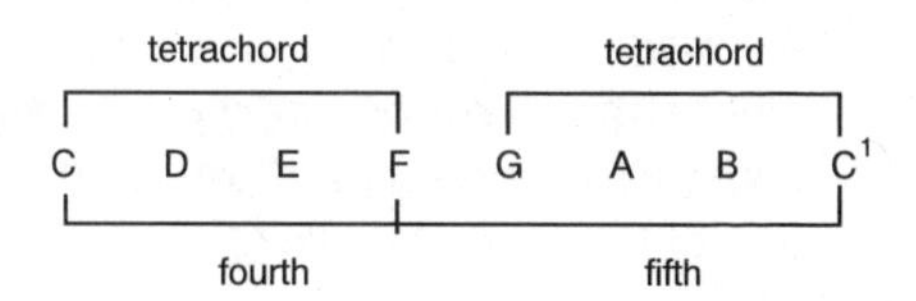

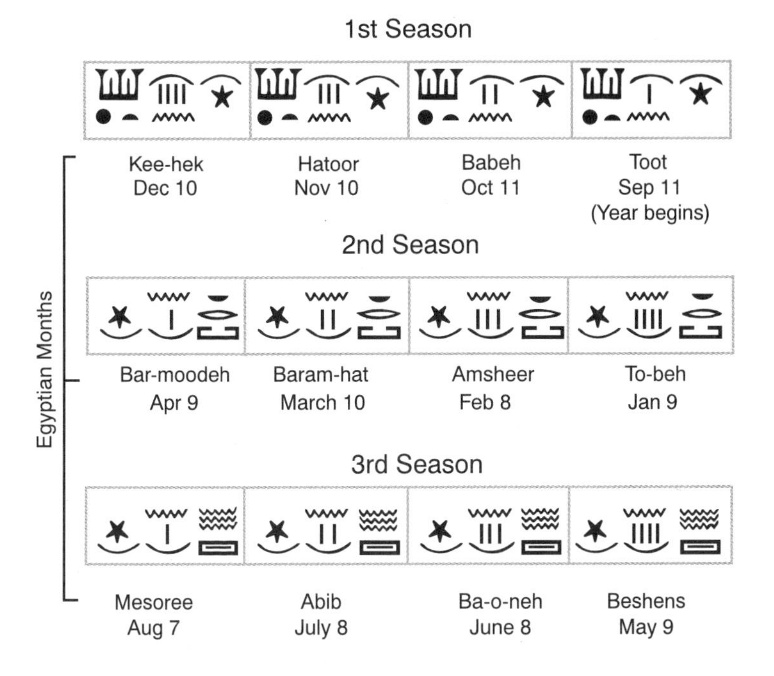

note. In the example shown here, the Fifth, in a descending scale, from C^1 is also *F* (C^1, *B*, *A*, *G*, ***F***).

- As noted earlier, the octave is the eighth natural tone of any given tone. In the case shown herein, C^1 is the octave of *C*, in an ascending scale.

3. **Tehuti** (Thoth), the patron of music, clearly establishes the intimate relationship between music and the triple progression of the three rhythmic seasons. Each Egyptian season consists of a tetrachord—a four-month period (each month consists of 30 days each). As stated on page 28, the tetrachord constituted the basis of music of the Ancient Egyptians.

The Complete Year

The Ancient Egyptians divided the year into 12 equal months of 30 days each; and added, according to Diodorus, 5 ¼ days to have a complete year.

> *The exact science of the stars were discovered, since their country [Egypt] enables them to observe more distinctly than others the risings and settings of the stars. Peculiar to them also is their ordering of the months and years. For they do not reckon the days by the moon, but by the sun, making their month of thirty days, and they add five and a quarter days to the twelve months and in this way fill out the cycle of the year. [Diodorus of Sicily, Book I, 50. 1-2.]*

It should be noted that the chronology of 3,000 years of Ancient Egyptian history, by modern Egyptologists, was made possible only because the Ancient Egyptians followed the Sothic Year of slightly over 365 ¼ days.

The Ancient Egyptians were able to construct a monument with perfect precision, to match their perfect calendrical calculations. At the Abu Simbel Temple of Ramses II, is a statue of Ramses II, located among other statues at the back of its sanctuary, 180ft (55m) away from the only opening to the Abu Simbel Temple. The rays of the sun have illuminated his statue, next to **Amon**'s statue, on February 22 (his coronation day) of each year for more than 3,200 years. The long duration of the shrine illumination is only possible because of the accuracy of the Ancient Egyptian Sothic calendar that followed the heliacal rising of **Sabt** (Sirius)—the Dog Star [also see page 36].

The ratio between 365.25 days and 360 days is 1.014. This ratio in the calendar has a similar musical equivalence, as we will find in chapter 9 of this book.

8

The Musical Dynamo (Auset and Ausar)

Panta (All) is a Derivative of Pente (Five)

The Ancient Egyptians expressed their knowledge of all subjects in a storyform fashion—as noted by all early Greek and Roman historians. The story of **Auset** (Isis) and **Ausar** (Osiris) was the Egyptian model, used to explain all facets of knowledge.

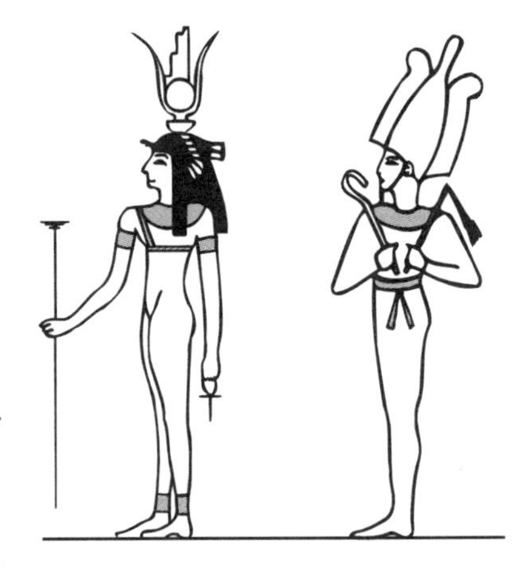

Auset
(Isis)

Ausar
(Osiris)

The role of **Auset** (Isis) and **Ausar** (Osiris), as it relates to the Egyptian three rhythmic seasons, is best described in

Diodorus of Sicily [Book I, 11. 5-6],

> *These two neteru (gods), they hold, regulate the entire universe, giving both nourishment and increase to all things by means of a system of three seasons which complete the full cycle through an unobservable movement. . . and these seasons, though in nature most opposed to one another, complete the cycle of the year in the fullest harmony.*

For the Egyptians, **Auset** (Isis) and **Ausar** (Osiris) regulated the music of the spheres. The universal harmonies are played out between these two primal male and female universal symbols of **Auset** and **Ausar**, whose heavenly marriage produced the son, **Heru** (Horus).

Plutarch wrote about the numerical significance of the Egyptian triad: **Auset, Ausar**, and **Heru**, in *Moralia* [Vol V], that the Ancient Egyptians equated the number two to **Auset** (Isis), three to **Ausar** (Osiris), and five to **Heru** (Horus).

> *Three (Osiris) is the first perfect odd number: four is a square whose side is the even number two (Isis); but five (Horus) is in some ways like to its father, and in some ways like to its mother, being made up of three and two. And* panta *(all) is a derivative of* pente *(five), and they speak of counting as "numbering by fives".*

The significance and function of number five, in Ancient Egypt, is indicated by the manner in which it was written. The number five in Ancient Egypt was written as two **I I** above three **I I I**, (or sometimes as a five-pointed star). In other words, number five (the son–**Heru**) is the result of the relationship between number two (the mother–**Auset**) and number three (the father–**Ausar**).

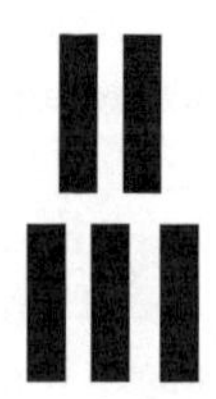

Musically, the ratio/relationship of 2:3 on the vibrating string and on the keyboard determines the vibration of the Perfect Fifth, reaching through five intervals (as shown here).

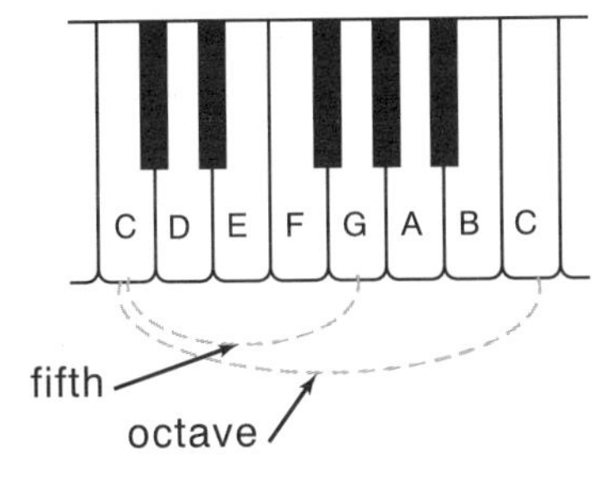

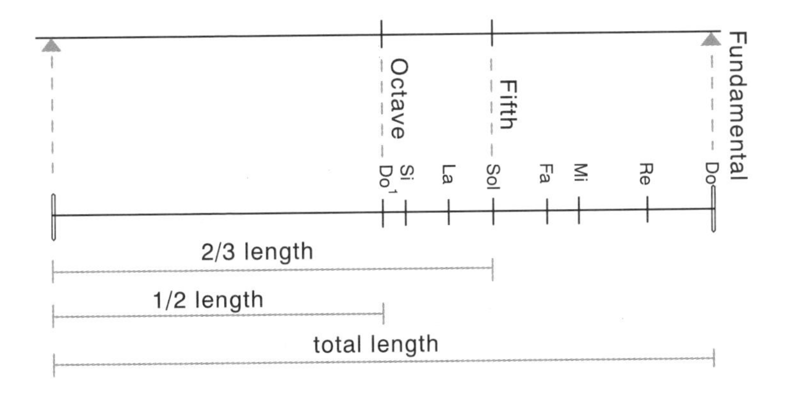

On a monochord, the sound of the natural Fifth is produced when the string is held down at a point that divides the string into a 2:3 ratio (as illustrated above).

The interval of the Fifth affords the strongest possible harmony between any two different tones. It is the first harmonic interval, to which all other harmonic intervals relate.

Plutarch stated the importance of the Fifth for the Egyptians, in his *Moralia* [Vol V]:

> *And* panta *(all) is a derivative of* pente *(five), and they [the Egyptians] speak of counting as "numbering by fives".*

Progression of the Harmonic Marriage (Counting by Fives)

The Ancient Egyptians counted "by fives", and the strongest and most natural progression from one harmony to another is the result of such development.

All musical scales are generated through progression of the Fifth. The form/relation of this first consonance is the first Fifth established by the heavenly marriage of **Auset** and **Ausar**. They in turn became a model to form, by a succession of similar relations, in a geometric progression.

The seven tones of the diatonic scale (*Do, Re, Mi, Fa, Sol, La, Si*) are the result of three progressions of Fifths. To simplify matters, we will illustrate the three progression of the Fifth on the keyboard, as follows:

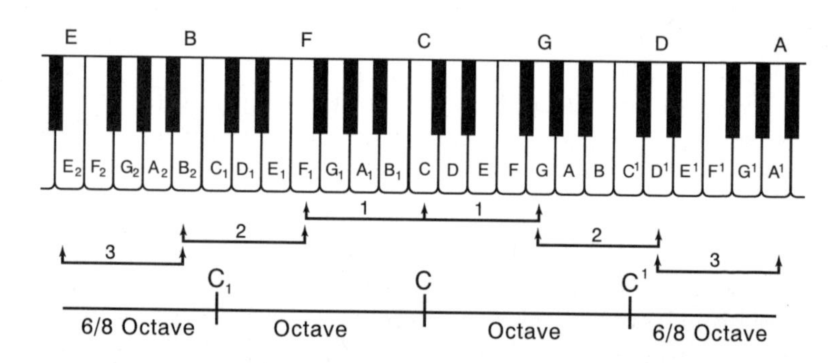

1. If we begin at any musical note, say the middle *C* (*Do*), as a generator, then find its two reciprocal Fifths, as shown above (*F* and *G*):

2. Second progression (from *F* and *G*) generates two more reciprocal Fifths (*B* and *D*), from the above two Fifths. This results in the pentatonic scale.

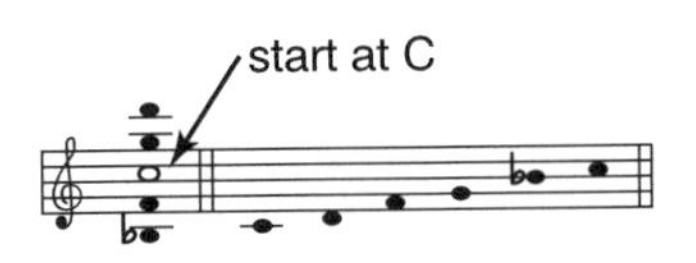

3. Third progression (from *B* and *D*): by adding two more reciprocal Fifths (*E* and *A*), the heptatonic scale is obtained.

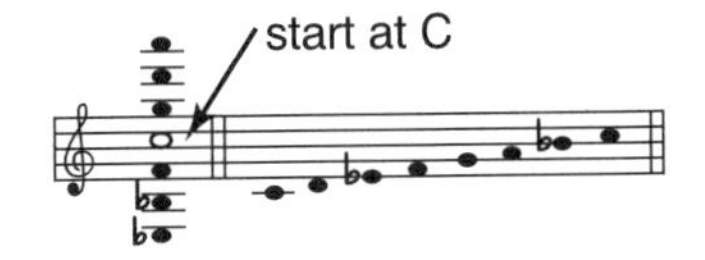

The diatonic scale is thus formed from any seven adjacent terms of a geometric series, ruled by the constant 3/2 or 2/3—the proportion of the Perfect Fifth. The seven natural musical tones are therefore obtained from the generative operation that extend three times, but no more.

To illustrate the cycle of the consecutive Fifths, which produce the diatonic scale on the keyboard, we imagine that the tones along the top line (*E B F C G D A*) are made into a circle with the tone *C*—the generator tone in our case—at the top. The result will be the common diagram known as the Cycle/Circle of the Fifths, as shown herein. From the note *C* (*Do*), we progress three times in each direction, to reach the seven tones of the diatonic scale.

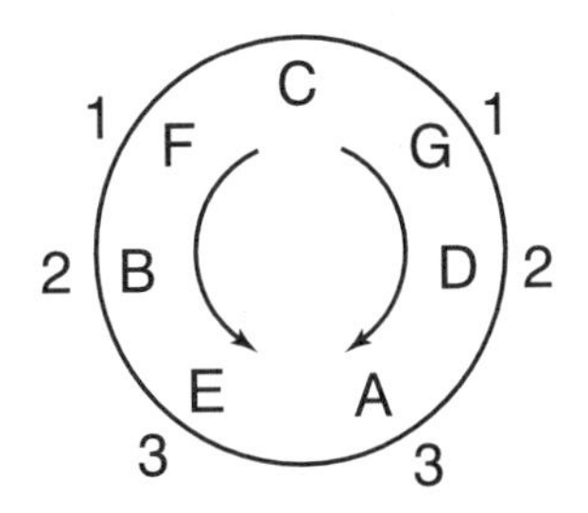

Harmonic progression along the cycle of Perfect Fifths is the most natural, and a succession of harmonies not in this relation has the character of a delay or suspension of this natural progression. From only one given Fifth, flows the whole musical system, which naturally must be in the same proportion as the first. There was no tampering with this proportion and no substitution for another one.

As noted earlier, the Egyptians understood that the number 2 (represented by **Auset**) and the number 3 (represented by **Ausar**) regulate the entire universe—including music.

All interval relationships can be reduced to 3x/2y or 2x/3y. The following are three examples to illustrate such a fact:

- The Perfect Tone = 8:9 = $2^3:3^2$
  This is also the perfect musical ratio, because it is the ratio between the reciprocals of 2 and 3 to their reciprocal powers of 3 and 2.

- The interval, *ebb*, as determined in terms of vibrations per second, is 65536/59049, which equals $2^{16}/3^{10}$.

- The interval, say 384 cents, as determined by vibrations per second, is 8192/6561 = $2^{13}/3^8$.

The progression by the Fifths to reach the seven tones of the diatonic scale, as illustrated on page 58 [below the keyboard], shows us that the generated (self-producing) Fifths never coincide with the progressing octaves.

The keyboard, however, cannot give us the true representation of the relationship between the progression of fifths and octaves. We therefore must follow the example shown on the monochord [on page 57] where it is shown that the Perfect Fifth is produced by 2/3 of the total length of the string and the octave at ½ of its length.

A progression by Perfect Fifths will mean finding the next Perfect Fifth at 2/3 of the original 2/3 of the length, ...etc. It is easy to see that any progress in fifths means multiplying by the ratio 2:3 by itself, and no power of 3 can ever coincide with a power of 2, which the octave requires.

We continue expanding by the fifths in both directions (up and down the scale). The successive transpositions of the scale produce numerous sharps and flats, arranged by fifths. The cycle of the self-producing Perfect Fifths are plotted along its length/circumference—the string is imagined to be looped in the form of a circle.

It was found that after 53 natural Fifths, any new Fifth expediently coincides with a prior existing Fifth. The increment between the 53 natural Fifths was/is called a *comma*. Accordingly, the Egyptians defined the tone system, with reference to the Circle of Fifths, on the basis of the unit of measure known as the *comma*, by subdividing the octave into 53 equal steps. This *comma* has a value of 22.6415 cents. (A *cent* is a standard unit for measuring musical intervals. An octave is equal to 1200 cents.)

It is interesting to note that the European treatises of the Middle Ages refer to this particular comma of 22.6415 cents as an *"Arabian Comma"*, even though no Arabian written documentation in the Arabized world ever mentioned it or used it—except for the Arabic speaking people of Egypt. As such, it can only be and was/is an Egyptian comma.

Analysis of Ancient Egyptian instruments is consistent with multiples of the Egyptian comma [see Part 3 and 4 of this book].

Each Egyptian comma consists of three equal parts, which the Egyptians called/call **buk-nunu**—meaning the *mouth of the baby*. This was/is an Egyptian term and not Arabic (a baby's mouth in Arabic is *Fam El Radee-a*). It should be noted that the division into thirds is consistent with the concept of the Fifth, since 2/3 of a comma is the Fifth within the comma.

The three **buk-nunu** in a comma are to be considered the Three-in-One—the Egyptian concept of trinity [read more about this subject in *Egyptian Cosmology: The Animated Universe*, by same author].

The size of **buk-nunu** is directly related to the very distinctive Ancient Egyptian calendar, as we will see in the next chapter.

Part

Musical Formulations

9

The Musical Measuring Unit

The Egyptian Musical Complement

As noted on page 54, the Ancient Egyptian calendar consists of 12 equal months of 30 days each (12x30 = 360 days), plus an additional period of 5 ¼ days, to complete the year at 365 ¼ days. The ratio between 365 ¼ days and 360 days is 1.014.

The same ratio was found in music, since 12 consecutive Perfect Fifths reach slightly farther than 7 octaves. The ratio between the 7 octaves and the 12 Perfect Fifths (in terms of vibrations per second) is:

$$(1/2)^7 \div (2/3)^{12} = 3^{12}/2^{19} = 531441/524288 = 1.014$$

The above similarity is not surprising, since the Ancient Egyptian system is based on the intimacy between astronomy (such as the calendar) and music. The Egyptians neither incorporated the extra 5 ¼ days into the 12 months, nor did they ever call the 5 ¼ days a month. For the Ancient Egyptians, musical sounds are the pulsation of the complete calendrical cycle.

The Egyptian Musical Measuring Units

The musical measuring units must be related to our capacity to hear and differentiate. We do not hear simple quantitative differences in soundwave frequencies, but rather the logarithmic, proportional differences between such frequencies.

The inner ear is shaped like a logarithmic spiral, to correspond to the way we hear. That spiral shape was noted in Egyptian medicine and jewelry—such as earrings.

To find out the value of the musical interval equivalent to the Egyptian calendrical complement of 5 ¼ days, we must find the logarithmic ratio between 365 ¼ days and 360 days, as follows:

$$\log 365.25 / 360 = \log 365.25 - \log 360 = 0.0062975$$

To convert this incremental interval into Western terminology of cents, will be:

$$0.0062975 \times 1200 = 7.557 \text{ cents}$$

It is this increment that an ear can differentiate. This increment is expediently equal to 1/3 the Egyptian comma of 22.64 cents.

This discreet increment of 1/3 comma was/is called **buk-nunu**, meaning the mouth of a baby, in Egypt. It is interesting to note that older Greek texts refer to the term, **buk-nunu**, even though it has no meaning whatsoever in their language, and no specific value was ever given to **buk-nunu**, in any Greek text.

It is also interesting to note that Philolaus, a Pythagorean from Tarentum, stated that *"the primordium of the whole tone is 27, the cube of 3"*. By dividing the whole tone (203.77 cents) by 27, the result is 7.55 cents—almost exactly like the value of 7.557 cents, based on the Egyptian system.

Again and again, one finds fragmented pieces of the complete knowledge of Ancient Egypt in Greek writings, which is indicative of the loss of the principle/basis of the Egyptian knowledge, as it transferred from one Greek generation to the next.

Analysis of the holes in found Ancient Egyptian wind instruments, and frets on found string instruments, as well as the ratio of string lengths in the harps, proves with consistency the use of these "unique" discreet increments of the Egyptian comma and **buk-nunu**.

An example is a common Ancient Egyptian interval of 11:12, which is equivalent to 151 cents = 6 2/3 commas = 20 **buk-nunus**. [More examples in Part 4 of this book.]

Western musicologists decided to sacrifice the well balanced natural sounds, for the sake of number simplification. Therefore, Western music is now based on "convenient" arithmetic and not on the true sound of natural tones. [More about this subject in Appendix A.]

In order for Western musicologists to write about the true natural musical tones, they came up with numerous and cumbersome terms, all of which can be reduced to multiples of the (one and only) Egyptian comma, such as:

1. minor semitone or *leimmas* of	90.56 cents =	4 commas
2. major semitone or *apotomes* of	113.21 cents =	5 commas
3. minor whole tone of	181.13 cents =	8 commas
4. major whole tone of	203.77 cents =	9 commas
5. natural Fourth of	498.11 cents =	22 commas
6. natural Fifth of	701.89 cents =	31 commas

The Comma, Buk-nunu, and the Siamese Twins

The musical comma is also consistent with the Ancient and *Baladi* Egyptians' belief that the universal energy matrix consists of nine realms: *seven heavens* (metaphysical realms) and *two lands/earths* (physical realms). The *two earthly realms* are commonly known as the *Two Lands/Earths*—the one we live in, and another one where each's twin (of the opposite sex) live. Each twin is subject to the same experiences from date of birth to date of death.

The seven higher realms are represented by the seven natural tones of the diatonic scale. The 8th realm is represented by the human being—the image of God. At the 9th realm is each's twin (of the opposite sex).

Musically, the ratio of 8:9 is called the *Perfect Tone*. The Perfect Tone equals a major whole tone of 9 Egyptian commas—in Western terms = 203.77 cents.

The excess between the twin souls at realm 8 and realm 9 is 1/9. The 1/9 ratio of the value of the Perfect Tone = 1/9 x 203.77 = 22.6411 cents, representing the Egyptian comma—the difference in vibration between you and your siamese twin, of the opposite sex.

The phenomenon of the musical siamese twins created the famed Ancient Egyptian twin-octave system. This is based on the fact that each natural tone has a mirror image (complementary opposite) tone—at a ratio equal to the Egyptian comma. By a shift of a musical comma in the internal structure of any scale, it will produce its "siamese twin" scale. The 2-octave scale is a twin scale—one is based on a sequence of natural tones and the other is based on the sequence of their opposite notes. In Western terms, the twin scales are called "plagal" and "authentic"!!

Shown below are the twin 24-note octaves, representing the 24 hours of the day. The ratio between each pair of twin notes is the Egyptian musical unit of a comma.

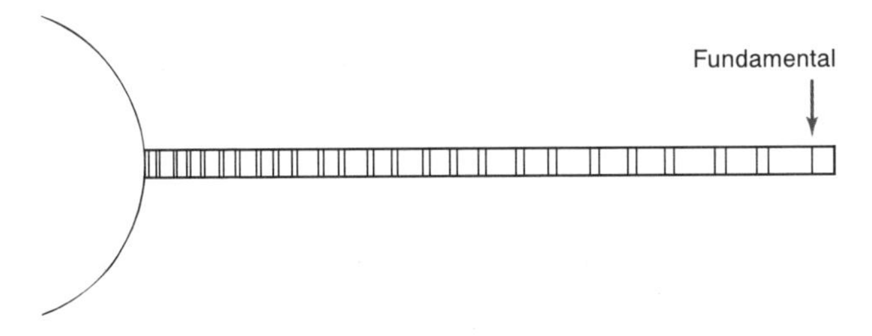

The ratio between both the 8th and the 9th realms to the Fundamental (The ALL) is 1:8 and 1:9. The difference between the two ratios is 1/8 – 1/9 = 1/72 = 0.014. This is the same excess over the Unity, as shown for the Egyptian calendar and its correspondence in music—the **buk-nunu** [see pages 65 and 66].

The Comma and the Musical Instruments

The Egyptian musical comma is an inevitable natural result of tuning and playing stringed musical instruments. Stringed instruments are basically tuned in two ways:

1. The cyclic (up and down) method, which applies to open (unstopped) strings of the instrument, yields Perfect Fourths and Perfect Fifths.
Tuning is done by selecting a string (*C*) and tuning another string to its upper Perfect Fifth (*G*), then reverting to (*D*) a Fourth down, and going up to (*A*) by another Fifth, and so on. This difference between a Fifth and a Fourth is called a major whole tone, which is equal to 203.77 cents (i.e. nine Egyptian commas). [An example of such a cyclic sequence in the Ancient Egyptian 17-tone framework is shown on page 73.]

2. The divisive method is utilized to tune instruments with defined necks (like a guitar). Tuning is accomplished by stopping strings along the neck at proportioned distances (by use of frets), as follows:
1/2 the length to get the Octave
1/3 the length to get the Fifth
1/4 the length to get the Fourth

When comparing the string vibrations of these two methods of tuning stringed instruments, we are faced with the following results:

	Cyclic	Divisive
C-D	203.77 cents (9 commas)	203.77 cents (9 commas)
D-E	203.77 cents (9 commas)	181.13 cents (8 commas)
E-F	90.56 cents (4 commas)	113.21 cents (5 commas)
Total:	498.11 cents	498.11 cents

The two tuning types show differences between *D–E* and *E–F*. The difference between the two methods yields two sizes of a whole tone (203.77 and 181.13 cents) and two sizes of semitone (90.56 and 113.21 cents). The difference between the two sizes is the Egyptian comma, for each of the intervals *D–E* and *E–F*.

The Egyptian orchestra tunes both types (cyclic and divisive) of string instruments by using the Egyptian **Ka-nun** (zither), which is the instrument that other instruments in the orchestra tune to, because it follows both principles at once: it has open strings that follow the cyclic system of tuning, while the melody string follows the divisive system. The melody string is fretted not by actual raised frets, but by marking the stopping places along the soundboard. [More about the **Ka-nun** on pages 106-107.]

10

The Musical Framework Varieties

The Overall Tone System

The Ancient Egyptian tone system was based on the integrity of the Perfect Fifth, which yields the division of the octave into 53 equal intervals (namely the comma)—each interval can be further divided into three **buk-nunu**. The comma is not an interval by itself, but a discreet increment in the whole spectrum of available tones. Out of this 53-tone compass came a variety of frameworks. Each framework constituted the raw material out of which various seven-natural-tone scales are formed for melody.

The octave-scale, whether diatonic, chromatic, or enharmonic, always consisted of eight notes and no more.

There were/are five basic intervals in use: 4, 5, 8, 9, and 12 commas. 13 or 14 comma intervals can be used under certain conditions. Commonly, the smallest interval was/is 4 commas (90 cents), and the largest is the augmented second of 12 commas (271 cents).

The two methods of tuning (cyclic and divisive) represent the two basic principles that have shaped the formation of all different scales. Each scale is based on the structure of its tetrachords.

- The cyclic principle is based on a tetrachord, consisting of 9, 9, and 4 musical commas [see table below].
- The divisive principle is based on a tetrachord, consisting of 9, 8, and 5 musical commas [see table below].
- The most popular mode in Egypt (*Bayati*) combines both a divisive tetrachord below and a cyclic pentachord above.

Based on the Ancient Egyptian musical unit of the comma, the player was/is able to perform in all three tetrachordal structures, i.e. allowing the semitone to stand wherever it is required within a tetrachord, as shown below:

	Cyclic			Divisive			
Semitone above	9	9	4	9	8	5	commas
	204	204	90	204	182	112	cents
Semitone in the middle	9	4	9	9	5	8	commas
	204	90	204	204	112	182	cents
Semitone below	4	9	9	5	9	8	commas
	90	204	204	112	204	182	cents

The Egyptians used different fretting techniques to diversify the scales that their instruments can play. Their fretting diversification allowed the playing of any/all of the three types of tetrachords [see fretting techniques on pages 110-11 and 116-17].

In this book, the 17-tone framework was selected to represent the cyclic principal, and the 22-tone framework to represent the divisive principle. Ancient Egyptian instruments were found to confirm the use of both frameworks (among others). [See *Instruments*, Part 4.]

The 17-Tone (Ausar) Cyclic Framework

The master 24x7 plan [pages 26-27] shows that the tones of the 10th, 17th, and 24th hour, of any day, are always the same. The 24th hour of the day signifies the end of the daily cycle. Because of the similarity of tone, both numbers 10 and 17 (in addition to 24) signify the end of a cycle. Accordingly, the Egyptians had/have cyclical frameworks of 10, 17, and 24 intervals.

Here we will touch base on the cycle of 17-tone framework, which is related to **Ausar** (Osiris), who represents the cyclical principle in the universe—the principle of coming and returning.

Seventeen tones per octave are arrived at when natural Fifths and Fourths are added and subtracted [see details on pg. 69]. It appears as a repeating sequence of 4,4,1 Egyptian commas. An example of such a cyclic sequence in the Ancient Egyptian 17-tone framework is shown herein.

Tone	Comma		Relative Cents
C			
	4	S	90.56
D-flat			
	4	S	90.56
E-flat-flat			
	1	c	22.64
D			
	4	S	90.56
E-flat			
	4	S	90.56
F-flat			
	1	c	22.64
E			
	4	S	90.56
F			
Total	22		498.11

S = Semitone
c = comma

This cyclic process yields the following framework:

SSc SSc SSc SSc SSc SS

where **S** is the (minor) semitone of 4 commas (90 cents) and **c** is the comma (22.64 cents).

The 17-tone framework can be utilized for building numerous scales by organizing the 17 steps in different ways. They are all based on two sizes of 9 and 4 commas. Here are three examples:

1. The common Western ascending *major scale*

C D E F G A B C¹

SSc	SSc	S	ScS	ScS	ScS	S	
9	9	4	9	9	9	4	commas
204	204	90	204	204	204	90	cents
T	T	S	T	T	T	S	

2. The common Western ascending *minor scale*

SSc	S	ScS	ScS	ScS	ScS	S	
9	4	9	9	9	9	4	commas
204	90	204	204	204	204	90	cents
T	s	T	T	T	T	s	

3. One of the most popular Egyptian musical modes is *Nahawand,* whose major form is arranged as follows:

C D E_b F G A_b B_b C¹

9	4	9	9	4	9	9	commas
204	90	204	204	90	204	204	cents

Note that:

S is the (minor) semitone of 4 commas (90 cents)
c is the comma (22.64 cents)
T is the tone of 204 cents.

The 22-Tone (Het-Heru) Divisive Framework

While the 17-tone framework is based on two different sizes (9 and 4 commas), the 22-tone divisive framework is based on three different sizes:

9 commas (204 cents), a major whole tone
8 commas (181 cents), a minor whole tone
5 commas (113 cents), a major semitone

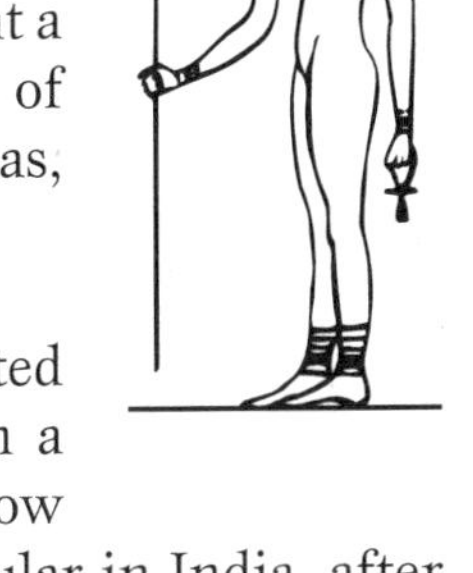

The number 22 is closely associated with **Het-Heru** (Hathor), as shown in the Hatshepsut Temple—dedicated to **Het-Heru**. Each terrace of this temple consists of a group of 22 columns on each side of the main causeway. It is also interesting to note that a tetrachord, which constitutes the basis of music, equals 22 Egyptian musical commas, which equals 498.11 cents.

Het-Heru (Hathor) was often depicted as a cow-headed woman, or entirely in a human form with cow ears. Both the cow and the 22-tone framework became popular in India, after trade contact with Ancient Egypt.

The ingredients of the 22-tone framework (9,8,5 commas) appeared in several arrangements according to the mode required. The two essential features of these scales are their shape and their transposition. The modal scales could be transposed to any pitch by changing semitones or major whole tones into minor whole tones, using only three elements:

1. a comma of 22.64 cents—the difference between the major and the minor whole tone (203.77–181.13 cents);

2. a set of three commas of 67.92 cents—the difference between the minor whole tone and the major semitone (181.13–113.21 cents);

3. a set of four commas of 90.51 cents—the difference between the major semitone and the comma (113.21–22.64 cents).

Consequently, the composition of

9 commas (the major whole tone) is	4 + 1 + 3 + 1
8 commas (the minor whole tone) is	4 + 1 + 3
5 commas (the major semitone) is	4 + 1

The D-scale can thus follow the sequence of the 22 elements:

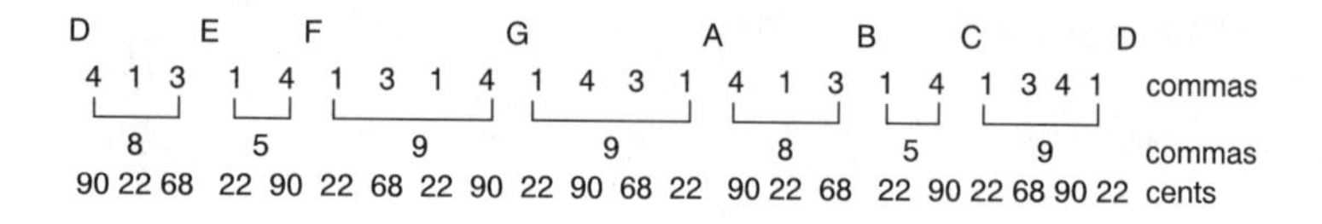

One of the main Egyptian musical modes is *Rast*, whose general form is arranged as follows:

C		D		E		F		G		A		B		C¹	
	9		8		5		9		9		8		5		commas
	204		181		113		204		204		181		113		cents

11

Musical Structure and Forms

Moods and Modes

We all recognize that certain musical modes make us happy, while others make us sad. The emotional power of different musical modes puts us in different moods, such as: exuberance, intoxication, exhaltation, religious devotion, love, playfulness, whimsicality, reflectiveness, seriousness, patriotism, sadness, longing, mournfulness, passion, serenity, calmness, joyfulness, despair, frenzied melancholy, mysticism, agitation, etc.

It is therefore that the composition of a melody/mode must follow certain design criteria, in order to meet the desired objective. This fact was first known and implemented in Ancient Egypt.

In the 4th century BCE, Plato recommended that the Ideal State be erected upon the foundation of music—a well-established system, based on a theory of the *ethos* of music—a theory of the psycho-physiological effects of music on the State and on man. Plato's recommendation was the adoption of Ancient Egypt's system and practices, as stated in Plato's *Collected Dialogues*, in *Laws II* [656c–657c]:

ATHENIAN: Then is it conceivable that anywhere where there are, or may hereafter be, sound laws in force touching this educative-playful function of the Muses, ***men of poetic gifts should be free to take whatever in the way of rhythm, melody, or diction tickles the composer's fancy in the act of composition and teach it through the choirs*** *to the boys and lads of a law-respecting society, leaving it to chance whether the result prove virtue or vice?*
CLINIAS: To be sure, that does not sound rational decidedly not.

ATHENIAN: And yet ***this is precisely what they are actually left free to do, I may say, in every community with the exception of Egypt****.*
CLINIAS: And in Egypt itself, now—pray how has the law regulated the matter there?

ATHENIAN: The mere report will surprise you. That nation, it would seem, long enough ago ***recognized the truth we are now affirming, that poses and melodies must be good****, if they are to be habitually practiced by the youthful generation of citizens. So* ***they drew up the inventory of all the standard types, and consecrated specimens of them in their temples****.*
. . . . . .

ATHENIAN: . . .in this matter of music in Egypt, it is a fact, and a thought-provoking fact, that ***it has actually proved possible, in such a sphere, to canonize melodies which exhibit an intrinsic rightness permanently by law****. . . .*
So, as I was saying before, if we can but detect the intrinsically right in such matters, in whatever degree, we should reduce them to law and system without misgiving, since the appeal to feeling which shows itself in the perpetual craving for novel musical sensation can, after all, do comparatively little to corrupt choric art, once it has been consecrated, by deriding it as out of fashion. ***In Egypt, at any***

rate, its corrupting influence appears to have been no-wise potent, but very much the reverse.
CLINIAS: That seems to be the state of the case from your present account.

ATHENIAN: Then may ***we say boldly that the right way to employ music and the recreations of the choric art is on some such lines as these?*** *When we believe things are going well with us, we feel delight, and, conversely, when we feel delight we believe things are well with us.*

The above scripts from Plato's *Collected Dialogues*, show how the Greeks considered Ancient Egypt to be the sole source of their Ideal Laws, as related to music (among other things). The Greek text above admits the following:

1. Only Egypt had sound laws that govern melodies and poses.

2. Only Egypt had an inventory of well-designed standard type modes/melodies and the regulations by which they are performed—time, place, and occasion.

3. Only Egypt had practiced their prescribed Ideal Laws for music, dance, poetry, etc.

The selection procedures of notes, modes, and movements were closely related to the Ancient Egyptian game of drafts. It is very common to find near Ancient Egyptian musical and dancing scenes a representation of a chess figure in the form of 'drafts' or 'checkers', indicative of this Ancient Egyptian branch of art of composition, which taught how to avoid and to play certain notes, how often each should be used, which one was to start, and which one to finish, . . .etc. The 24x7 Master Plan [on pages 26-27] serves as the main reference guide.

Design Characteristics of Modes

In order to achieve a specific emotional outcome, the composition of a mode must project specific characteristics, with its peculiar flow of energy. Each mode has a structure and tension of its own. The main design ingredients are: *rhythm*, *meter*, and *pitch*. The traditional patterns (modes) are characterized not only by their heptatonic scale but also by their particular tempo, general curve, emotional atmosphere, and melodic turns. The composer's freedom is limited to the few traits that do not interfere with the immutable qualities of the pattern.

Each mode is formed of its own unique combination of tones and rhythms—a succession of tones of differing pitch. Generally, ascending and descending motions (steps and/or leaps) balance one another. The restoration of balance is frequently delayed or not immediately apparent.

Melodies therefore always have a definite relationship to some accepted scale. The real foundation of melodic motion is the scale of natural tones. Modes can be put together from established frameworks [see previous chapter]. Each mode is based on a heptatonic scale (sequence of seven natural tones), i.e. each consists of five whole tones and two semitones, arranged and rearranged in many ways. The Egyptian musical increment—the comma—allowed the Egyptians the ability to lower/raise pitches in several ways, in order to diversify the succession of the seven natural tones.

As noted on page 50, **Tehuti's** number—eight—is the rhythmic number in the universe. The normal musical sentence is that of eight measures, frequently but not necessarily divided into two half sentences of four measures each. There are other sentences or phrases that are shorter and longer; these are brought about by omissions or overlappings, or by extensions, repetitions, or expansions. Eight measures is the norm.

Likewise, the octave-scale, whether diatonic, chromatic, or enharmonic, always consisted of eight notes and no more—either as two disjoined tetrachords, or joined + 1 note, or overlapping tetrachords + additional notes—but always eight notes to the octave. With these variations, some scales were tense and others relaxed, some disjunct and others conjunct, some pure and others mixed, some "plagal" and others "authentic", some denoted structures and others keys—just to mention a few of the endless possibilities.

As stated on page 28, the tetrachord constituted the basis of Ancient Egyptian music. Each tetrachord expands a Fourth. The natural Perfect Fourth has a definite size, which is 22 Egyptian commas (498.11 cents).

Each tetrachord contains two whole notes and one semitone. The inner organization of the tetrachord decides the gender and mode. The size and arrangement of the two whole tones and one semitone, within a tetrachord, varies in two main ways:

1. The location of the semitone in a tetrachord determines the location of its energy center. Three types of organization within a tetrachord are shown on page 72.

2. The sizes of steps/intervals within the tetrachord determine the gender/genus of the mode/scale. In all cases, a tetrachord/natural Fourth is equal to 22 Egyptian commas. [The main variations of sizes are shown on page 72.]

There are numerous aspects to be considered in musical composition. This book will not get into all their details. However, another important aspect of composition, namely the tempo, will be discussed in general terms, beginning on page 90.

The Written Sounds

The Ancient Egyptians were extremely literal people who documented all aspects of their civilization—in written form. Therefore, it should not come as a surprise that they also wrote musical sounds as they did their spoken sounds (language). For the Ancient Egyptians, music and language are two sides of the same coin. The written symbols (letters) are sonic pictures, i.e. each spoken letter has a specific vibration (pitch), just like the musical alphabet [see page 49].

The Ancient Egyptian language is ideal for musical writing, because its symbols (letters) can be written in any direction, and therefore their sequence can be inverted like a scale—up-down, right-left, or vice-versa. [More was presented on page 49.]

Plato acknowledged that the Ancient Egyptians notated their musical tunes, in his *Laws* [656-7]:

> *. . .postures and tunes that are harmonically pleasing. These they* ***prescribed in detail and posted up in the temples*** *. . . . .*

The Ancient Egyptian language consists of hundreds of symbols. Some of them may be equated to alphabetic representations. [It should be noted that Western academia has arbitrarily and incorrectly selected some of the Ancient Egyptian symbols and declared them to be the "Egyptian alphabet".] In addition to the most commonly used symbols (alphabets), there were several hundred so-called syllabic symbols, as well as a great number of determinative signs.

In music that accompanies singing, every musical note

is written separately, to correspond to a syllable of the text. In other words, each musical note has an equivalent syllable, and vice-versa.

All early Greek and Roman writers affirmed that there were basically two forms of Ancient Egyptian writings: hieroglyphs (sacred script) and the abbreviated form of the hieroglyphic symbols, characterized as a script without pictorial forms (a type of shorthand symbols). Western academia arbitrarily splits the non-pictorial type into two forms—hieratic and demotic.

The Greeks used the same letters and sequence of alphabet that was used in Ancient Egypt, and is still used in Egypt now, to write music. The musical notes in ancient Greece followed the Ancient Egyptian alphabet order/sequence, which is *A B G D H W Z H T Y K L M N*. . . . . The number and order of this alphabet does not follow the character or sound or sequence of the Greek (or the Arabic) alphabet. *Baladi* Egyptians are familiar with this purely Egyptian alphabet. Incidentally, the Ancient Egyptian documents, labeled "Ptolemy" by academia, followed the same Ancient Egyptian alphabet and sequence, as did the writings of St. John of Damascus.

In addition to the Ancient Egyptian musical alphabets, the Ancient Egyptian musical notation system found its way a long time ago into Greece. This was the result of the Egyptian **Dor-ians** [see chapter 4]. Western academia acknowledges that the Greeks used a notation system of non-Greek origin. Some described it as an "archaic language". Others described it as a "mutilated foreign alphabet".

François Joseph Fétis, an accomplished musicologist, discovered the roots of the Greeks' notation symbols to be the demotic form of the Ancient Egyptian writing.

F. J. Fétis states in his *Biographie Universelle des Musiciens et Bibliographie Générale de la Musique* [Bruxelles, 1837, tome I, p. lxxi.],

> *"I have not the least doubt, that this musical notation [used in ecclesiastical music by the modern Greeks] belonged to ancient Egypt. I have in support of my opinion the resemblance borne by the signs in this notation, erroneously attributed to St. John of Damascus, to those of the demotic, or popular characters of the ancient Egyptians. . . . .*
> *. . . . .*

M. Fétis continued by pointing out the resemblance existing between numerous symbols employed by the Greeks to determine the duration of notes, and certain characters of the demotic symbols, in a lengthy and detailed analysis [read more of the portion of the English translation of M. Fétis' text in Carl Engel's book, *The Music of the Most Ancient Nations*, pg 271-2], M. Fétis did not hesitate to conclude:

> *"After this detailed analysis of the system of notation employed in the music of the Greek Church, and after comparing its signs with those of the demotic character in use among the Egyptians, can we for a moment doubt that the invention of this notation is to be ascribed to that ancient people [the Egyptians], and not to St. John of Damascus. .*
> *. . . . .*

M. Fétis's detailed analysis and conclusion proves without the shadow of any doubt that the Greeks borrowed the musical notation of the Egyptian demotic symbols. This is an additional piece of evidence that the characteristics of the Egyptian music—via the **Dor-ians**—have been preserved in the Greek references.

Another musicologist, namely Charles Burney [see bibliography], noted that an inventory of the available notations show that the Ancients utilized more than 120 (actually 125) different characters for sound only. When taking into account the time (or tempo) variation, as it relates to the different modes and genera, the sound characters were multiplied to more than 1620 (actually 1625). Burney described this huge number as consisting mostly of lines, curves, hooks, right and acute angles, and other simple figures, placed in varied positions, a form of what he described as "mutilated foreign alphabet". The symbols of the so-called "mutilated foreign alphabet" are actually the Ancient Egyptian demotic symbols, as noted by M. Fétis.

By checking the Ancient Egyptian hieroglyphic and demotic scripts, one will easily find huge similarities with even present-day musical notations of flags, keys, notes, ties, slurs, dots, arcs, such as:

- prevalence of dots, dashes, > , < , b, p, and ovals.
- different sizes and colors of circles and sections thereof, i.e. ½ and ¼ circles as well as arcs.
- lines (vertical and horizontal), crosses, diagonals, hooks.
- combinations of above.

It was, however, easier to learn and follow the Ancient Egyptian notation system, because it was consistent with their language. The present-day Western notation system is comprised of cumbersome abstracts that must be memorized without thinking.

12

The Musical Performance

The Harmonic Merit Hand

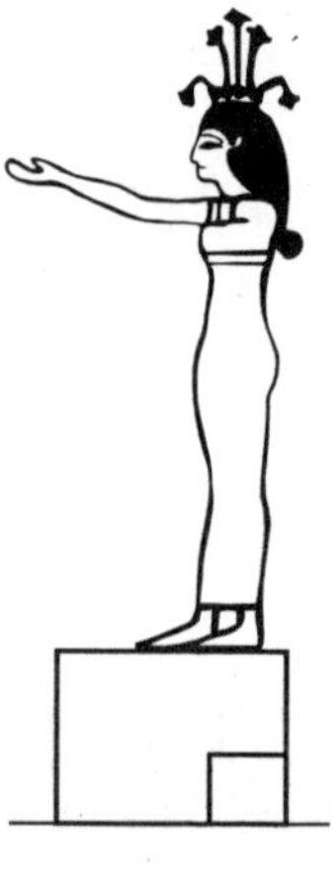

Merit is the name of an Ancient Egyptian **netert** (goddess), who was considered to be the personification of music. **Merit's** major function was to establish cosmic order by means of her gestures, and as such, **Merit** is the cosmic conductor/maestro who manages the notes and the flow of musical performances.

This understanding of the role of the hand in Ancient Egypt made Plato define music itself as *"the art of guiding the singers of a chorale"*. The Greeks have ascribed their hand waving signs to the Ancient Egyptian practice of music.

The hand of **Merit** is the universal symbol of action. Musically, the fingers control the sound emitted from musical instruments. How you place fingers determines the tones. Therefore, fingers are the most logical way to express, write, and instruct music.

Each finger has a different effect in playing a string instrument (a similar analogy is also applicable to wind instruments). The same note, produced on a different string, has a different color. Additionally, when the same string is pulled by the forefinger or the middle finger of the right hand, the sounds produced are characterized by a different timbre. The technique by which these variations in timbre and color are effected produces at least 26 varieties of the vibrato alone. As a consequence, a certain note took its name from the string plucked or deadened by this finger. As such, fingers have often been used to describe the technique of striking, among the expressions of instrumental playing.

In Ancient Egypt (like present-day), tones, strings, scales, and melodies are all related and therefore expressed by a particular finger, *asba* (plural: *asabi*). In Egypt (Ancient and *Baladi*), this conventional "finger movement" mode has been all that is needed to identify the different modes. In the early years of the post-Islam era (after 640 CE), the Arabized countries used the same Egyptian finger expressions. After a few centuries, they began using an Arabic term, *maqam,* instead of the Egyptian term of *asba*.

Fingers were also used to measure distances in Ancient Egypt. The main standard linear measure was the **mh** (cubit)—the length of the forearm from the elbow to the tip of the middle finger. One Egyptian cubit measures 1.72 feet (0.5236m). The Egyptian cubit was further divided into seven handbreadths/ palms of four digits (finger breadth) each, or 28.

In the consistent and coherent Egyptian way of thinking, the four fingers (like a tetrachord) produce sound and measurement.

Ancient Egyptian tombs and temples yield several series of choreographic, rhythmic and melodic hand signs that correspond to certain signs of chironomids. The tones are presented by different positions of the arms and fingers (forefinger against the thumb, the stretched out hand, etc), resulting in an absolute correspondence between tonal steps of the Ancient Egyptian musical system and hand signs.

The chironomid presided over the musical ensemble and, by a range of gestures, determined the pitch and intervals on which the musicians based their performance. The details of this examination are reported in a special study [H. Hickmann, *The Chironomy in Ancient Egypt*, Magazine of Egyptian Language and the Antique 83, 2, 1958.].

Symphonic and polyphonic variations are depicted in musical scenes of Ancient Egyptian buildings from the Old Kingdom (4500 years ago), with a director to guide the total ensemble by means of visible gestures. One or more chironomids were depicted to signify the type of performance. It must be noted that depiciting more than one chironomid for one instrument is symbolic of the action intended—in the Ancient Egyptian artistic representation.

Egyptian chironomids guided the musicians in basically three different ways, to provide single, double, and triple tonalities, as follows:

1. The chironomids are indicating identical hand signs,

thus the musician(s) is/are playing in unison.

2. The chironomids are indicating different hand signs, thus the musicians are playing a chord. The following are two examples:

a. In the tomb of Ti [Sakkara, Old Kingdom], we have two illustrated chironomids giving different hand signals, for a single instrument (harp)—representing two different sounds, i.e. portraying an example of polyphony.

This depiction of two chironomids is indicative of double tonality—which could be either consecutive or simultaneous.

b. Playing a chord with three different tones is depicted [shown below] in Nencheftka's tomb [5th Dynasty, Sakkara, now in Cairo Museum]. Three different hand signals are shown by the depicted chironomids.

Another example of polyphony composed of three different tones is presented in a musical scene from a relief from the tomb of Nekauhor [Sakkara, 5th Dynasty, presently at the Metropolitan Museum of Art, New York].

The Rhythmic Timing

As stated in chapter 6, the Ancient Egyptians identified the three elements that constitute an orderly flow of sound (regular pitch, noise, and muting). These three categories enable us to identify the duration of each sound, as well as the rest time (silence) between consecutive sounds.

Music, like language, is read in pattern, not individual units, i.e. we read words, not letters. Understanding music/words/phrases depends upon sensation and memory; for we must not only feel sounds at the instant they strike the instrument, but remember those that had been struck before, in order to be able to compare them together. The time element separating consecutive tones is the organizing factor in hearing, feeling, and comprehending the intent of music or spoken words/phrases.

The emotional effect of music depends largely upon the type of rhythm that it employs. Rhythm means flow: a movement that surges and recedes in intensity. The flow of rhythm assumes many forms in music. Much of the color and personality of music comes from its rhythm. This may be the contrast of strong and weak impulses, long and short note values, low and high pitch, slow or fast, even or uneven, with accents frequent or infrequent. Combination of these elements give rhythm its character.

Maintaining a specific rhythm was/is very critical, since the strict union of poetry and music among the Ancient and *Baladi* Egyptians seems to have been almost inseparable. As such, any deviation from the specified time or rhythm not only destroyed the beauty of the poetry, but sometimes even the meaning of the words of which it was composed. A change in vowel pronunciation makes it a different sound—different vowel—and hence a different word.

In addition to musical performance, rhythmic timing is also applicable to:

- Vocal music, where each note is written separately, corresponding to a syllable of the text. [More in chapter 18.]

- Dancing. It is through Ancient Egyptian dancing scenes that the rhythmic patterns of the accompanying texts were discovered.

The rhythm of the human being is mostly related to the heart pulse. Rhythm has an effect on the heart, and is measured against it as well. We have a clock built into us—the pulse—whose normal rate is about 72 beats per minute. [See also the relationship between the number 72 and **buk-nunu** on page 69.] It is by this yardstick that we judge rapid or slow events—their tempo. When the musical tempo varies from the heart pulse (faster or slower), then it will cause unnatural excitement.

Slower music = quietness, softness, sorrow
Faster tempo = happiness, joy, vitality

The numbers 2 and 3 are the numbers of **Auset** (Isis) and **Ausar** (Osiris), the regulators of the entire universe [see pg 56]. As such, practically all rhythmic organization is based on one of two general schemes: the *binary*—strong alternating with a weak beat, or *ternary*—strong followed by two weak beats. One or the other of these types underlies the rhythmic framework of every composition. The underlying binary or ternary rhythm is known as the *fundamental rhythm*. Subdivisions of these beats that appear within the general framework are called the *subsidiary rhythm*.

The numbers 2 and 3 are related to the natural breathing rhythm and therefore are reflected into the binary and ternary method of time measurement in musical performance. When a person is in a quiet sleep, the time between expiration and inhalation is twice as long as that between inhalation and exhalation. It is the idea behind all musical forms. The in-and-out, the alternation of tension and relaxation, governs all further manifestations.

Beating time in music is quite important, because if a musician (not percussionist) falls out of time, the music sounds off and the ear tends to stop listening and to drift. Beat is the constant pulsation. It acts as a ruler by which we can measure the duration of a note and the time between notes. Time beating could be accomplished by any of the following ways:

1. Musicians learn to keep time with the aid of onomatopoeic syllables—quietly. The correspondence between syllables and musical notes makes this method of time-keeping very natural.
Singing to/with music follows the same pattern, and can be accomplished in two ways: 1) by using certain syllables for the duration of the note, and/or for time in between notes; 2) or an even or alternate recurrence of numbers, by counting to oneself.
Usually, two sizes of syllables are utilized: short and long, i.e. a long/longer vowel, at a ratio of 2:1. These two basic elements are used in numerous variations for variable meters—the sequence of beats and rests contained in each time segment.

2. Foot beating is depicted in Ancient Egyptian musical scenes, as a method of keeping time. [Also see page 94.]

3. In many musical representations in the Ancient Egyptian buildings, musicians are accompanied by a person clapping, or using clappers, to keep the musicians in time. [See chapter 16 for additional information.]

4. The Egyptians utilized/utilize the drum patterns of small hand drums, the goblet drum (*tabla/darabukkah*), the frame drum (*riqq* or *tar*), or the pair of kettle drums (*naqqarat*) to regulate the time. [See chapter 16 for additional information.]

5. Classical Egyptian practices had two kinds of beats working in combination, silent and audible.

- Silent gestures were used in Ancient Egypt, in various ways by giving signals, such as: lifting the forearm, turning the palm either up or down, and stretching or doubling up the fingers; one hand held partly out with thumb and forefinger forming a circle and other fingers held stiffly, while the other hand is placed on the ear or on the knee in a relaxed position, with the palm upward or downward. The thumb may be up, or bent against the forefinger.

[A few examples of time-beating, as shown in tombs in Sakkara from the Old Kingdom.]

In performing these movements, the hands alternated from member to member: with the right hand; the left hand, and both hands.

The fingers, too, alternated. In duple time, the four parts of a period were denoted by pointing first with the small finger and successively adding the ring finger, the middle finger, and the index finger.

- Audible beats were also provided by: snapping the fingers; slapping (as the thigh) with the right hand or with the left hand; or slapping with both hands.

  In the tomb of Amenemhet at Ta-Apet (Thebes), dated ca. 1500 BCE, is depicted a conductor standing before and facing the performers, pounding time with her right heel and snapping both her thumbs and forefingers.

Part

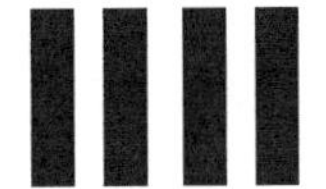

Musical Instruments

13

The Wealth of Instruments

The Egyptian Instruments

The archeological and traditional Egyptian history of music is much more abundant than in any other country. The wall reliefs of the Ancient Egyptian temples and tombs depict numerous types and forms of musical instruments, the technique in which these instruments were to be played and tuned, the ensemble playing, and much, much more.

These musical scenes visibly show the hands of the harp player striking certain strings, and the wind instrument players playing certain chords.

The distances of the lute frets clearly show that the corresponding intervals and scales can be measured and calculated. The positions of the harpists' hands on the strings clearly indicate ratios such as the Fourth, the Fifth, and the Octave—revealing an unquestionable knowledge of the laws governing musical harmony. The playing of musical instruments is controlled by the conductors' hand movements, which also help us identify certain tones, intervals and functions of sound.

In addition to the numerous representations of musical scenes pictured in temples and tombs from all periods throughout Egypt's dynastic history, we also have access to hundreds of various Ancient Egyptian musical instruments that have been recovered from their tombs. These Egyptian instruments are now spread in museums and private collections throughout the world. Most of these instruments were found to be carefully and individually wrapped in cloth, before they were buried.

All these findings, together with the early historian writings of Egyptian musical heritage, as well as the traditions of modern Nile inhabitants, corroborate to provide the most authentic case of the musical history of Ancient Egypt.

Unfortunately, much of this CLEARLY EGYPTIAN evidence has been distorted, time and time again throughout history, by Western academia. [More about the historical distortion by Western academia can be found in the Appendices of this book.]

General Characteristics of Egyptian Instruments

1. Some tombs yielded actual instruments that were never depicted in reliefs of temples or tombs, such as cylindrical bass drums. Only the Egyptian instruments that were related to the function of the operation of temples and tombs were depicted in the reliefs. Many other instruments that were not a part of these religious activities in temples and tombs were not represented.

2. It should also be emphasized that most Ancient Egyptian tombs were robbed, mostly by foreign invaders,

and only a few instruments were left behind. It is these "few" (even though a very large quantity compared to any other country) that we have some records of. Accordingly, one should not conclude that because certain instruments were not found in the survived temples and tombs (of which most were destroyed) that they didn't exist in Ancient Egypt.

3. The depicted musical scenes in Ancient Egyptian tombs, as well as instruments found from the Old and Middle Kingdoms, indicate ratios between the open strings of the harp, the densely ordered frets on the long necks of string instruments, as well as the measurements between the fingerholes in wind instruments that reveal/confirm:

- **a.** Several types of musical scales that are based on the unique Egyptian musical comma and its triple parts of **buk-nunu**.
- **b.** Narrow-stepped scales were common from the earliest known Egyptian history (more than 5,000 years ago.
- **c.** Playing and tuning techniques of string instruments to provide solo and chordal playing of instruments.
- **d.** Playing techniques of wind instruments that provide small increments and organ effect.
- **e.** The use of both the cyclic (up-and-down) method, and the divisive method. [See chapters 9 and 14.]

4. The Ancient Egyptians were/are famed worldwide for their mastery of the playing techniques of their musical instruments. The skill of the Egyptians, in the use of these instruments, was affirmed by Athenaeus, who stated (in his texts [iv, 25]) that both the Greeks and "barbarians" were taught music by Egyptian natives.

After the demise of the Ancient Egyptian Pharaonic Era, Egypt continued to be the learning center for music, for the Arabized/Islamized countries.

5. The "decorative" elements of the Ancient Egyptian string instruments have vital significance. The ends of these instruments are "decorated" with the heads of **neteru** (gods/goddesses), animals, humans and birds. The swan is found prominently in many instruments. The swan was regarded by the Ancient Egyptians as a bird sacred in two capacities: 1) as being like the crow and raven, gifted with the spirit of prediction; and 2) for his extraordinary vocal powers. The sweetness of his song, especially at the approach of death, was not only extolled by all the poets of antiquity, but by historians, philosophers, and sages.

6. **Ma-at** is found prominently in numerous instruments to represent her function as *balanced equilibrium*. Her name was mistaken to be the name of several instruments, by Western academicians. Names of instruments given by Western academia are arbitrary. Ancient Egyptians did not use abstract names, they used descriptive adjectives for everything to describe their functions. It is therefore very common to find several terms ("names") for a person, an instrument, or anything. [More about naming and names in Ancient Egypt in *Egyptian Cosmology: The Animated Universe*, by same author.]

7. The cosmic conscious Egyptians changed emphasis in

EVERYTHING in their life in order to attune to the changes in the zodiac ages. The utilization of some instruments more than others in different eras was a direct response to cosmic changes and nothing else. [See *Egyptian Cosmology: The Animated Universe*, by same author, for these Egyptian practices.]

It is absurd to arbitrarily assume that the prominence of an instrument in a certain era is due to Egyptian importation, especially when there is no evidence that such an instrument ever existed in the alleged region.

All early Greek and Roman writers reported that Egyptians never adopted others' ways. [Refer to chapter 22, *The Beat Goes On*.]

7. The presence of hieroglyphs in the shape of musical instruments (much older than 5,000 years) attest to their Egyptian origin.

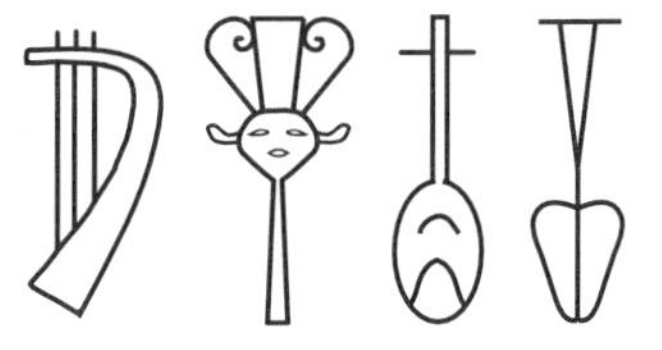

The Musical Orchestra

Musical instruments differ in compass, variety of strength of a single note, accent value, survival value, speed of articulation for a repeated note and how many notes each instrument can play at once. As such, a variety of instruments were utilized by the Ancient Egyptians, to provide a complete system/range of musical sounds.

It should be noted that the overview of Ancient Egyptian musical instruments in this book is limited to instruments that can be compared with present-day instruments.

Some of the instruments of the Ancient Egyptians differ too much from the present day classification to be classed with any of them.

Musical bands varied in Ancient Egypt. Smaller and larger ensembles were employed for various purposes, as evident from depicted musical scenes in the Ancient Egyptian buildings. It is sufficiently evident, from the sculptures of the Ancient Egyptians, that their musicians were acquainted with the triple symphony—the harmony of instruments, voices, and of voices and instruments. The playing of musical instruments was controlled by the conductors' movements of hands (chironomids). Their hand signs show a variety of playing: unison, chord, polyphony, ...etc., as stated in chapter 12.

The Egyptian orchestra/ensemble consisted generally of the four instrument groups:

1. String instruments with open strings, like tri-gonon, lyre, harp, ...etc. [See chapter 14.]

2. String instruments with stopped strings on a neck, like the tanboura, guitar, oud/lute, etc. [See chapter 14.]

3. Wind instruments like the flute, pipe, etc. [See chapter 15.]

4. Percussion instruments like drums, clappers, bells, ...etc. [See chapter 16.]

The following chapters detail found and depicted Ancient Egyptian instruments, as categorized above.

14

Stringed Instruments

General

The Ancient Egyptian stringed instruments consist of basically two groups:

1. those with open strings: lyres, harps, zithers, etc. This group is usually tuned by ear in a *cycle* of fifths and fourths.

2. those with stopped strings: instruments with well defined necks, such as tanbouras, guitars, etc. This group is governed by the *divisive* method of tuning.

There are however lyres, harps, and zithers with strings occasionally stopped, and tanbouras with open strings, as explained in the **Ka-nun** playing technique [see chapter 9], and as will be explained in the harp playing techniques on pages 110-111.

[See the tuning methods of the different types of stringed instruments on pages 69-70.]

Lyres

Ancient Egyptian lyres have a yoke-shaped frame consisting of two arms and a crossbar that projects from the upper side of the body. There were two main types of lyres in Ancient Egypt:

1. Asymmetrical shape, which has two divergent asymmetrical arms, an oblique crossbar, and a soundbox.

2. Symmetrical rectangular shape, which has two parallel arms, a crossbar at right angles, and the soundbox.

The quality of the sound of both types was influenced by the soundbox, which was basically square or trapezoid in outline.

Many Egyptian lyres were of considerable power, having 5, 7, 10, and 18 strings. They were usually supported between the elbow and the side, and played with the hand and/or with the plectrum. The plectrum was made of tortoise-shell, bone, ivory, or wood, and was often attached to the lyre by a string.

The numerous depictions of lyre playing techniques corresponds with the technique of present-day playing. The lyre was held at a slant, or even horizontal, away from the player. The pressure of the fingers stretched the strings and thus altered the pitch. The right hand scratched with a plectrum over all strings at once, while the fingers of the left hand, stretched against the strings, deadened those that were not wanted.

The Egyptian lyres had a compass of several octaves, which contain the unique Egyptian musical increments.

Smaller tones were produced similar to the harp playing techniques described on pages 110-111.

There are perfectly preserved wooden lyres [now in the Berlin and Leiden museums]. In the Leiden collection, the two limbs of the lyres are adorned by horses' heads. Their design, form, principle, and alternate long and short strings, resemble some of those depicted in several Ancient Egyptian tombs.

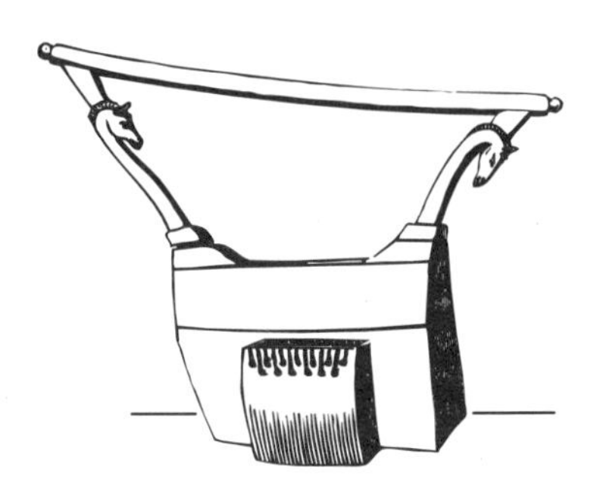

The following are additional examples of depicted/ found Ancient Egyptian lyres:

- **Bes**, recognized since the pre-dynastic era [prior to 3000 BCE], is shown in a bronze statuette striking the strings of an asymmetrical lyre with a plectrum [now in the Cairo Museum, cat. #41736].
- A symmetrical lyre was identified by Hans Hickmann in a 6th Dynasty tomb [2323-2150 BCE, Sakkara].
- Asymmetrical lyres from the Middle Kingdom [2040-1783 BCE] are depicted in the tombs of Beni Hassan.
- An asymmetrical lyre was found bearing an inscription to Amenhotep I [16th century BCE].
- A symmetrical 14-stringed lyre is depicted, in the tomb of Kynebu [dated to the 12th century BCE], reminiscent of surviving Ancient Egyptian lyres [now in the Berlin and Leiden Museums].

Tri-gonon/Tri-Ka-Nun (Zither)

Flavius Josephus, in his volumes *History of the Jews*, stated that the Ancient Egyptian temple musicians played an *enharmonic triangular instrument (órganon trígonon enarmónion)*. The *trígonon* consists of two terms, *tri* and *gonon*. The term *tri* is indicative of the form and nature of this unique Egyptian instrument, which is:

- shaped in a triangular form, which some call trapezoidal, because the shortest string must have a length in order to produce a sound.
- the arrangement of the strings—in triplets. Each of the three strings have different thicknesses, and all three are tuned in unison.

The Greek term, *tri-gonon*, has closely preserved the Egyptian term, namely the [triangular-shaped] **Ka-Nun**. The trigonon/tri-**Ka-Nun** is commonly known in Egypt as **Ka-Nun**—an Ancient Egyptian term meaning the *personification/embodiment* (**ka**) of the *world* (**Nun**).

The **Ka-Nun**/qanun has played an extremely important role in Ancient Egypt, as testified by Flavius Josephus. Even today it is the heart—so to speak—of any Egyptian musical ensemble.

- There is an Ancient Egyptian raft zither at the Museum for Ethnology and Prehistory [Hamburg, Germany].
- **Ka-Nun**/Kanoon was mentioned by al-Farabi [10th century CE] to be an instrument of 45 strings (15 triplets) that was already in existence in his time.
- **Ka-Nun** was never referred to as an instrument of any other origin but Egypt, and Egypt is still recognized as the best builder of this instrument. The instrument's

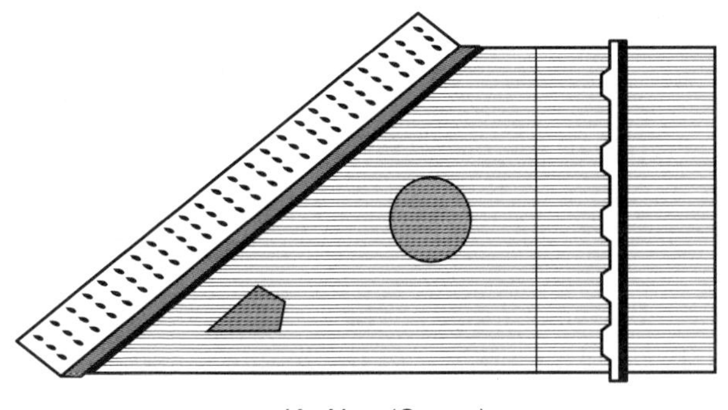

Ka-Nun (Canon)

name, Ka-Nun/*kanon*, appears in one of the oldest stories of *The Arabian Nights*, the tale of Ali ibn Bakkar and Shams al-Nahar (169th night), which is ascribed to the 10th century. An epithet to its name, *misri*, indicates *Masr* or Egypt as its home.

The present form of the Ka-Nun is a flat box with a triangular-shaped body of strings. It varies from 21 to 28 triple strings (total of 63 to 84 strings), but the most common consists of 26 triplets (78 strings). Each triplet is tuned in unison.

The strings are plucked with tortoise-shell plectra, which are affixed to rings that are worn on the right and left index fingers. The right hand plays the melody and the left hand doubles it in the lower octave, except for those passages where it stops a string to raise its pitch. The instrument has detachable metal bridges that can be placed beneath the strings to alter their length and therefore their tuning. Playing techniques can also follow the same techniques for lyres and harps [more details on pages 110-111].

The Ka-Nun was/is a major instrument in the Egyptian ensemble. The Ka-Nun player is positioned in the middle of the musical band. He/she was/is the tune setter, and as such, all the instruments in the ensemble are tuned to the Ka-Nun. It is the canon, the rule, and the ruler. [Also see page 70.]

Harps

The Ancient Egyptian harps varied greatly in form, size, and the number of their strings. They are represented in the ancient paintings with 4, 6, 7, 8, 9, 10, 11, 12, 14, 17, 20, 21, and 22 strings.

The harp was thought to be especially suited for temple service. It was even shown in the hands of the deities themselves.

There were basically two types of harps:

1. the small portable (shoulder) harp (shallow arch). Shoulder harps are found in large numbers in museums throughout the world. Like all instruments of the sort, they had a setting that could be moved from front to back, from top to bottom or vice-versa. It was a kind of suspension rod for the strings, which allowed for a quick tuning to different pitches.

2. the larger, arched (bow) harp or angular harp. There have been several variations of the large harps in Egypt, such as in their structures and sizes, depending on the string holder and whether it lies on the top or bottom, and whether the resonator is straight-lined or bent.

   [Shown herein is a scene from the tomb of Amenemhet, Beni Hassan, 12th Dynasty.]

There is barely any difference between the bow (arch) and angular harp, as far as their sound is concerned.

A few examples of Ancient Egyptian harps are listed below:

- The tomb of Debhen from Giza [ca. 2550 BCE] depicts two bow harps, with well defined sound bodies.
- A huge bow harp is depicted in a relief from the tomb of Seshemnofer [Giza, 5th Dynasty, ca. 2500 BCE].
- A bow harp is depicted in a scene from the tomb of Ti [ca. 2400 BCE] at Sakkara.
- A bow harp is depicted in the Ptah-hotep tomb [ca. 2400 BCE]. The scene shows 2-tone playing [also see page 89].
- A harp is depicted in a relief from the tomb of Nekauhor [2390 BCE, Sakkara, now at the Metropolitan Museum of Art, New York]. The scene shows 3-tone playing of music [also see page 89].
- 5 harp players in polyphonic playing are depicted in Idut's tomb, [ca. 2320 BCE] at Sakkara.
- The wife of the deceased Mereruka [ca. 2290 BCE] is shown playing a large harp in Mereruka's tomb in Sakkara. She is playing two different strings of the harp—polyphony [also see page 89].
- A bow harp is depicted in Rekhmire's tomb [ca. 1420 BCE], in **Ta-Apet** (Thebes). The string pegs are neatly depicted in the form of a modern trumpet mouthpiece.
- A bow harp is depicted in the tomb of Nakht [15th century BCE], **Ta-Apet** (Thebes).

- Two musicians are shown playing two huge forms of the bowed harp in the tomb of Ramses III [1194-1163 BCE], **Ta-Apet** (Thebes). Because of the two harp players, this tomb was called *The Harpers Tomb*, and the harps are known as *Bruce's Harps*. One harp is shown herein. [The other harp is shown on page 113.]

- Ramses III is depicted offering a harp, in the sanctuary of the temple of Medinet Habu, in western **Ta-Apet** (Thebes).

Harp Playing Techniques

The strings of harps were always plucked with the fingers or a plectrum.

Ancient Egyptians were familiar with a whole series of playing techniques, as evident from tombs throughout Ancient Egypt's dynastic history. Both one-handed and two-handed playing techniques are presented, as follows:

1. One-Handed Playing

With harps, every note has an individual, 'open' string. The one-handed technique is based on the *divisive* method of obtaining musical notes by stopping the string at certain proportional lengths. When this method is applied to the harp, only one hand is manipulating (shortening) the string for a specific ratio, which allows the other hand to pluck the shortened string (providing the note).

In order to locate the exact proportioned length of the string, and to ensure a firm contact at the proportional point, one of the left-hand fingers stretches and presses the string for the proportioned distance against a rod-shaped object (like a fingerboard), thereby shortening (stopping) the vibrating length of the string. The left hand was guided by frets, which were loops tied about the fingerboard at given points. This shortened length of this particular string can then be struck to produce the sound.

This one-handed technique allows an unlimited possibility of tones.

There are many examples shown of harpers performing this technique. They clearly show that the plucked string forms a slight angle. Examples:

- In a relief [shown herein] from tomb 11 in the **Ta-Apet** (Thebes) area [New Kingdom 1520 BCE], a harper shortens the string with one hand, and plucks with the other. The bent string is clearly shown.

- In Idut's Tomb [ca. 2320 BCE], two of the five depicted harpers pluck with only the right hand, while the left one holds down the string.

2. Two-Handed Playing

The two-handed technique is based on the ability to pluck each open string with one of the player's fingers. Both hands can pluck the strings either individually, simultaneously, or one after the other, i.e. playing a chord or polyphony. Unwanted strings can be further dampened (muted) with the palm of the other hand.

The All-Encompassing Capacities of Ancient Egyptian Harps

The numerous variety of the Ancient Egyptian harps reveals the wealth of their music producing capabilities. The following overview is based on the ratio between open strings only.

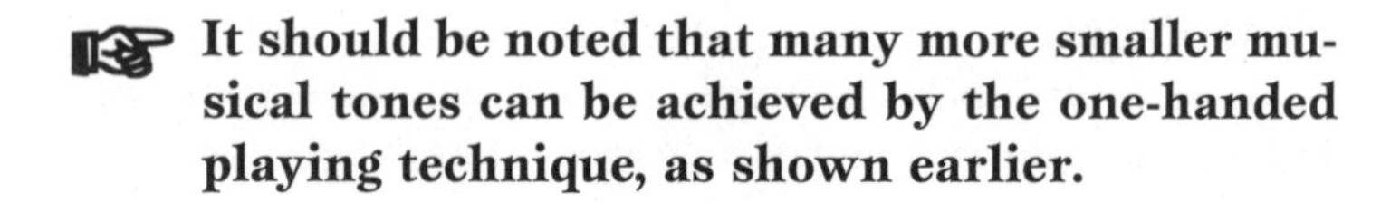

☞ **It should be noted that many more smaller musical tones can be achieved by the one-handed playing technique, as shown earlier.**

1. With harps of 4 to 22 strings, some harps would have been capable of producing a wide range of notes for several octaves. The ratio between the shortest and longest is 1:3 to 1:4 (i.e. 1 to 2 octaves). With the one-handed playing technique [pages 110-111], unlimited possibilities of various tones and octaves can be achieved.

2. The intervals of Fourth, Fifth, and Octave were the most common in Ancient Egyptian representations. Curt Sachs [in his book, *History of Musical Instruments*] found that out of 17 harpists represented on Egyptian art works with sufficient realism and distinctness to be reliable records, seven are striking a Fourth chord, five a Fifth chord, and five an Octave chord.

3. The ratio between the shortest and the longest string of several Ancient Egyptian harps is about 2:3. As this interval is divided between five strings, the scale would provide a range of tones between half and full tones. On harps with ten strings, this would give an average interval of a (minor) semitone (90 cents = 4 commas).

4. One of the two harps found in Ramses III's tomb has 13 strings, where if the longest string represented *pros-lambanomenos*, or *D*, the remaining 12 strings would more than supply all the tones, semitones, and quarter-tones, of the diatonic, chromatic, and enharmonic genera, within the compass of an octave.

The tuning of this 13-string harp can furnish the four tetrachords, *hypaton, meson, synemmenon*, and *diezeugnenon*, with *proslambanomenos* at the bottom:

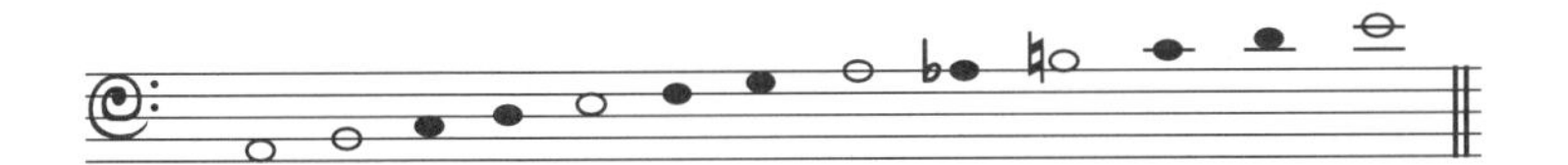

5. The most frequently depicted harps were found to have seven strings, and according to Curt Sachs' study of the Egyptian instruments, the Egyptians tuned their harps in the same diatonic series of intervals.

6. An Ancient Egyptian harp with 20 strings [found in Ta-Apet (Thebes)], appears to have had the pentatonic scale running through four octaves. And the harp with 21 strings [in the Paris Museum], probably had the same order of intervals, with the addition of the keynote at the top.

Tanbouras (String Instruments with Neck)

The tanboura/tamboura is basically a string instrument with a well defined long neck, which is used to stop the string at any desired length, before striking it.

The tanboura is known by many other "names", such as *tamboura* or *nabla*. [See item #5 on page 100, regarding "names" in Ancient Egypt.] We will use *tanboura* here as a *family name* for string instruments with a defined neck. Such a family of instruments includes (but is not limited to) short neck lutes, long neck guitars, ...etc.

This tanboura-type instrument appears on numerous wall paintings, sculptured panels, scarabs, sarcophagi, and as an ornament on vases and boxes; and representing in hieroglyphics the single attribute: *good/beautiful*.

A figure of the tanboura-type instrument is found among the Egyptian hieroglyphs, dating it to more than 5,000 years ago. The figure depicts two, and sometimes four, tuning pegs.

In Ancient Egypt, tanbouras led the religious processions, validating its present nickname as *King of Instruments*. The tanboura with the short neck (known now by its Arabic name *oud*) continues to serve musical instructional purposes, acoustic demonstrations, musical theory, and is the cornerstone of concert, family, and folk music, including theater, movie and radio presentations.

The Ancient Egyptians utilized tanboura-type string instruments in an unlimited variety, providing variation in sound and design, such as:

A. **Body Shapes:** The body shapes varied from an oval to one with sides slightly curved like present-day guitars or violins. They were also shaped like a tortoise shell or pear, with a flat or slightly rounded back. They all had sounding holes—through the top or the body of the instrument.

B. **Strings and Tuning:** Tuning pegs are clearly shown on the hieroglyphic symbols. Found instruments indicate the use of 2-5 pegs, which usually have tassels dangling from them. The tuning pegs of some tanbouras are shaped like the letter *T*, and are inserted from the front or the side. Many instruments were buried in the tombs without pegs or strings.
Ancient Egyptian tanbouras had strings of two, three, four, five, or six, which were made of catgut, silk or horsetail threads. Strings were produced in different thicknesses. When all the strings of an instrument were of the same thickness, a tuning peg was needed for each string. When the thicknesses of the strings were varied proportionally, so as to provide the different musical ratios between the strings, fewer tuning pegs were required. As such, a tuning peg may control several strings (of variable thicknesses) that can be tuned in unison. The tanboura-type instrument was played with a plectrum or bow.

C. **Length of Neck:** Some instruments have the long neck like a guitar, or the short neck like a lute or *oud*.
The length of the short neck was as short as the body of the resonator [see page 117 and 119].
The long neck was as long as 47 inches (120cm), as in Harmosis' instrument [see page 121].

D. Fretting: The musician shortened the vibrating lengths of the strings by pressing them against the neck, to produce notes of different pitch. To assist in stopping the required proportioned length of the string—to provide a specific pitch—most instruments came with frets in a variety of forms, in order to allow for flexibility of performance.

Since frets restrict the player to specific positions, stringed instruments played by the well trained musicians were often left without frets, so that the finger could glide freely along the fingerboard.

The frets of Ancient Egyptian instruments either:

1. were easily shifted, by moving the fretting bands.
2. were lightly marked. The strings were thin enough and sufficiently high above the fingerboard to be conveniently driven up in pitch by adding pressure.
3. were only marked at some big intervals by bands, to outline the overall parameter, to allow both guidance and flexibility. In addition, there were mobile frets that, together with these frets, divided the octave into smaller increments, such as 10, 17, 22, or more sections.

   An example is shown herein from the tomb of Nakht-amun in Ta-Apet (Thebes) [14th century BCE, Tomb 341].

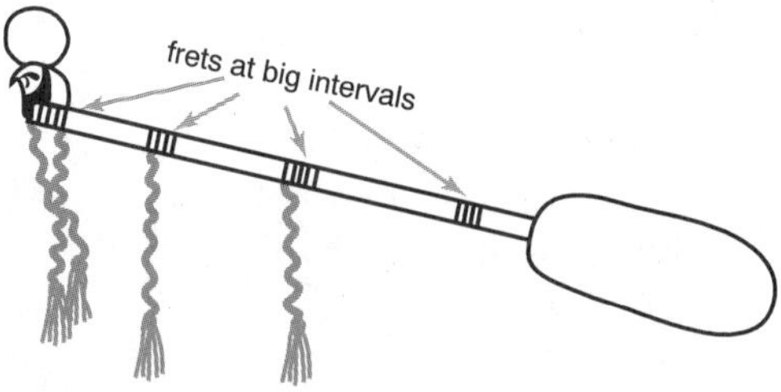

   [See more examples on page 122.]
4. were sometimes limited to the upper half of the neck, or sometimes extended down the neck to the body of the instrument. [Some examples are shown on page 122.]

The flexibility of fretting techniques allows for:

1. the selection of any of the three types of tetrachords [see page 72] and frameworks [see chapter 10].

2. increasing the instrument's capacity to produce numerous notes, and consequently reduces the necessity to use more and different string instruments—in the musical ensemble—to provide the different tetrarchords and modes.

Two-String Tanboura

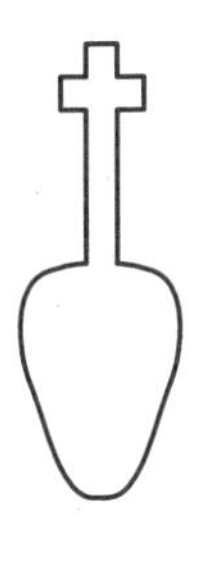

Two strings were capable of producing a great number of notes. For instance, if these two strings were tuned Fourths to each other, they would furnish that series of sounds called heptachord, consisting of *two conjunct tetrachords*, as *B, c, d, e; E, f, g, a*; and if the strings of this instrument were tuned Fifths, they would produce an octave, consisting of two *disjunct tetrachords*.

This very Ancient Egyptian instrument (resembling the hieroglyphic symbol) proves that the Ancient Egyptians had discovered the means of extending their scale, and multiplying the sounds of a few strings, by the most simple and practical means.

Examples from the numerous Ancient Egyptian representations include:

1. A two-stringed tanboura with frets is depicted in a music scene in **Ta-Apet** (Thebes) [Tomb 80, ca. 1450 BCE].

2. A two-stringed instrument appears in a music scene of a tomb in **Ta-Apet** (Thebes) [Tomb 341, 14th century BCE].

Three-String Tanboura

Three strings were common for the Ancient Egyptian tanboura-type instruments.

They were tuned in the Fourth, Fifth, and Octave. When each string is tuned in Fourths, the tanboura can reach a 2-octave range.

An example of this instrument was found in the tomb of Harmosis [see page 121].

One of the most popular types in Ancient Egypt was the *te-bouni*, a banjo-like, three-stringed instrument with moon-shaped body and parchment head.

Four-string Tanboura

The Ancient Egyptian obelisk [now in Rome], which was built ca. 1500 BCE, depicts a tanboura with four tuning pegs [shown herein].

Four-stringed tanboura-type instruments may have all their strings of the same thickness, in which case they were/are tuned in Fourths, to provide a compass of one or two Octaves.

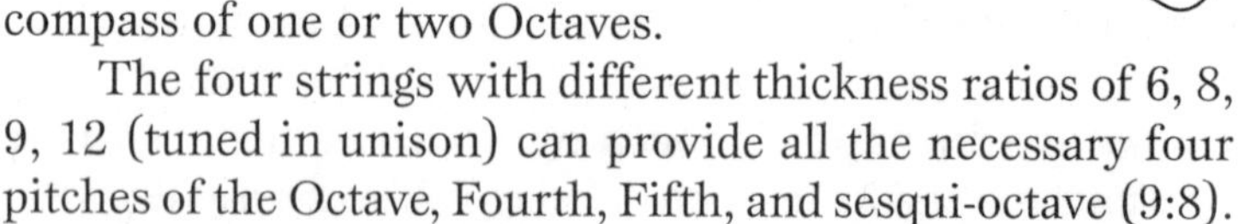

The four strings with different thickness ratios of 6, 8, 9, 12 (tuned in unison) can provide all the necessary four pitches of the Octave, Fourth, Fifth, and sesqui-octave (9:8).

The 4-stringed instrument continues to be popular in present-day Egypt.

Short-Neck Lute (present-day *oud*)

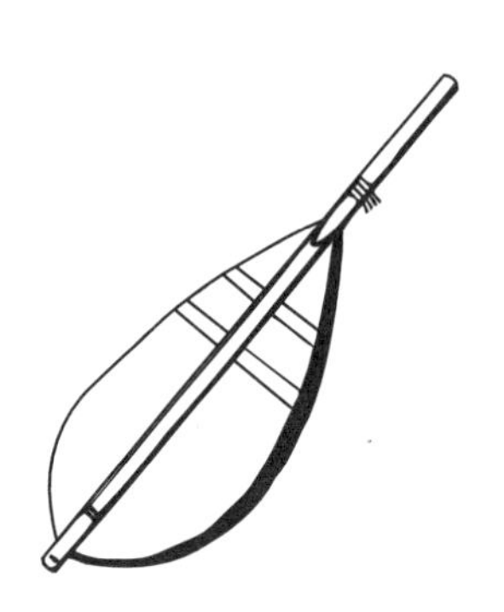

Ancient Egyptians were familiar with a type of short-neck lute with a sturdy pear-shaped body and a broad fingerboard. The number of strings ranged from two to six strings. Two lutes of this type came from Ancient Egyptian tombs in **Ta-Apet** (Thebes) [dated ca. 16th century BCE, now in the Berlin Museum], and are 14" (35cm) and 19" (48.5cm) long. The small one [shown herein] had 2, or possibly 3, strings. The larger one had 4 strings.

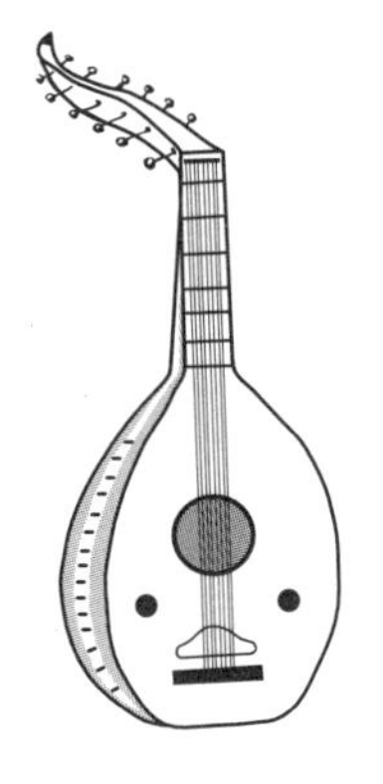

The most popular of this type had/have four strings. Along with the frets, the instrument was/is able to provide the most popular 17-interval framework. This instrument is known today in the Arabized/Islamized countries as *oud*.

In addition to the above Egyptian instruments [now at the Berlin Museum], some other examples of this Ancient Egyptian instrument include:

- A short neck type lute is shown in a statuette of a lute player [New Kingdom, ca. 3500 years ago, now at the Cairo Museum, cat. #773].

- A statuette made of burnt clay shows a musician playing a short-neck lute. [19-20th Dynasty, Cairo Museum, cat. #38797.]

The Egyptian Guitars

The Egyptian guitar consisted of two parts: a long flat neck, or handle, and a hollow oval body. They are found depicted in numerous Ancient Egyptian tombs from all eras.

Four Ancient Egyptian strongly notched guitar-like instruments were found in the Qarara region, which dated to the Middle Kingdom [wrongly and arbitrarily dated by others to the 6th century CE. No such instrument was/is related to the church in Egypt]. In addition to one at Heidelberg, a complete instrument of that kind is found in the Cairo Museum, another in the Metropolitan Museum of Art in New York, and a smaller one in the collection of Moeck, Celle. They are designed for three to six strings.

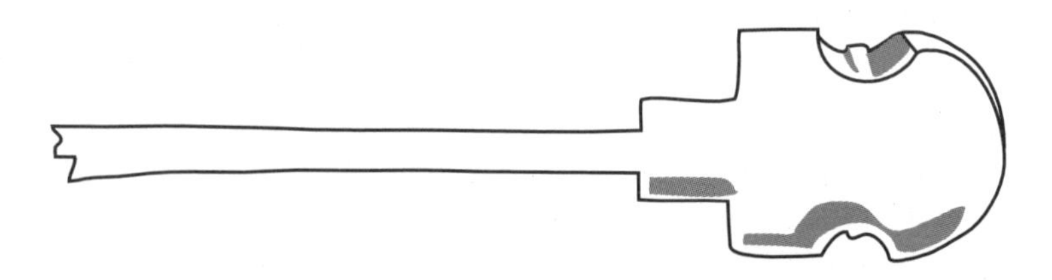

All these instruments are made of one piece, only the necks of the larger examples are elongated by pieces of extension, and all the instruments were provided with numerous frets.

It is from an ancient instrument of this kind, sometimes called *cithara/kithara*, that the modern name guitar (chitarra) has been derived. Their strongly lifted and tied up sound-producing body was the archetype for the present-day guitar.

A Few Examples of Tanboura Variety

1. A tanboura-type instrument with seven frets is depicted in an Ancient Egyptian tomb from the Old Kingdom [ca. 4500 years ago, now in the Berlin Museum]. The performer was therefore able to produce eight different intervals on each string. The spaces between the frets are painted in various colors.

2. Long-necked guitars, characterized by a long, extending and slightly laced resonance body are depicted in a music scene from the tomb of Pahekmen. **Ta-Apet** (Thebes) [Tomb #343], 18th Dynasty.

3. A tanboura-type instrument with a 25" (62cm) neck was found in Tomb 1389, **Ta-Apet** (Thebes). [18th Dynasty, ca. 16th century BCE, now in Cairo Museum, cat. #69420.] The body is made of tortoise shell.

4. A large form of a long neck tanboura-type instrument, with a 47" (120cm) long neck, was found in the tomb of Harmosis, [Thebes at Dêr el-Bahari, 16th century BCE, now at the Cairo Museum, cat. #69421]. The instrument was made of a wooden, half almond-formed resonator. Its three strings were tied at the bottom end to a specifically made projection. Then, the strings ran along a higher mechanism that could be moved back and forth.

5. Two tanboura-type instrument players are shown on a section from a wall painting in the tomb of Rekhmire [ca. 1420 BCE, **Ta-Apet** (Thebes)].

6. Long-necked instruments are played by a group in a part of a procession, depicted at the Temple of Luxor, from the time of Tut-Ankh-Amen [ca. 1350 BCE].

7. A music scene from the tomb of Nebamun [Ta-Apet (Thebes), 15th century BCE, now in the British Museum] depicts two types: a long-necked guitar with long almond-shaped resonator, and one with a rounded resonator. The latter appears to be made of a tortoise shell.

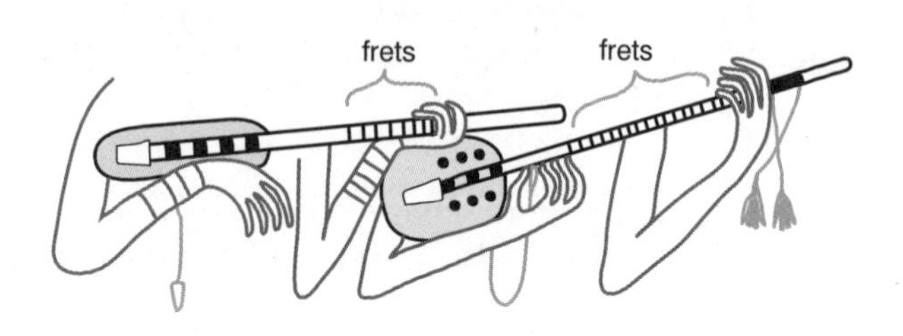

Both instruments here are provided with fingerboards. One has 8 visible frets, which begin halfway down the neck. The other has 17 visible frets.

8. A long-neck tanboura-type instrument is depicted in Ta-Apet (Thebes) [Tomb 52, 15th century BCE], named after Nakht. The instrument has nine frets on its long neck, marked with bands. This instrument provides the span of a 10-interval framework [see page 73], which was in use in Ancient Egypt. The measurement of the visible (not blocked by the player's hand) distances between some depicted frets yield the following intervals (in cents): 134–114–341–202–272, i.e. 6–5–15–9–12 Egyptian commas. The measured intervals are again consistent with the Egyptian musical comma as the measuring unit.

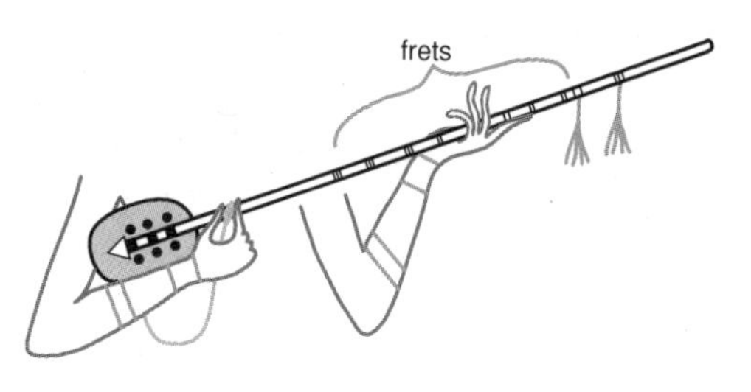

It also shows the twin-octave system, a comma apart.

Bowed Instruments (Kamanga, Rababa)

There are several types and forms of bowed instruments, but they all follow the principle of the freely swinging resonance strings that can be bowed or plucked. Bowed instruments had/have 1, 2, 3, or 4 strings. Two and four strings are the most common.

The strings of the instruments, as well as the bows, are made of horsetail hair. Horses have played a major role in the musical life of Ancient and *Baladi* Egypt. Several Ancient Egyptian instruments are adorned with figures of horses. The hair from horsetails—abundant and available to all—was/is used to produce music.

The typical way of playing all types and sizes of bowed instruments by the Ancient and *Baladi* Egyptians is to rest the body of the instrument on the thigh or on the floor, and not under the chin, no matter how small the instrument is. The Egyptian way allows more control and the ability to turn (pivot) the instrument to produce the exact desired pitch and its duration.

Ancient Egyptian tombs show this Egyptian style of playing bowed instruments. In the tomb of Rekhmire [15th century BCE, Ta-Apet (Thebes), Tomb #100], a female musician is depicted bowing the stringed instrument.

A similar scene is found in another tomb, where the instrument is resting on the player's thigh.

Bowed instruments are called *kamanga*. They had/have squared or rectangular bodies, and somewhat rounded backs.

The form and structure of the *kamanga* is the same as the later, present-day violin.

Bowed instruments with two strings are called *junior kamanga* or *ra-ba-ba*—an Egyptian term meaning the *Twin Soul* (**ba-ba**) *of the Creator* (**Ra**). The Twin Soul (**ba-ba**) is represented with two strings.

The *rababa* is a fiddle with a long fretless neck, and may be plucked or bowed. It has a short, narrow and cup-shaped body.

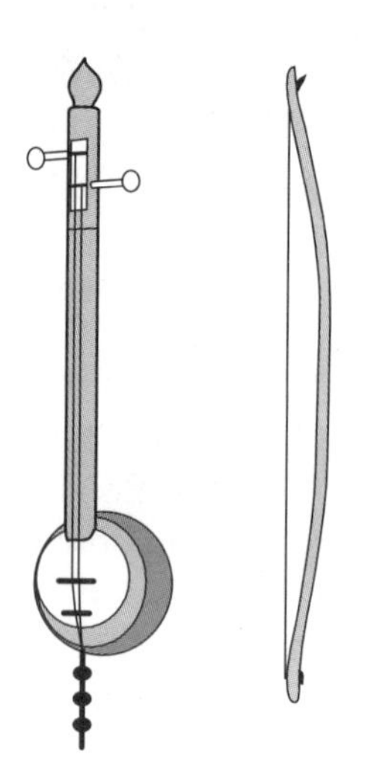

Rababas are very cheap to make as both the strings and the bow are made of horsetail hair. The resonating body can be a carved coconut shell or wooden.

The bows of both *rababa* and *kamanga* are made of a flexible elastic, slightly bent rod and horsehair.

Bowed instruments (such as *kamanga* and *rababa*) accompanied/accompany storytellers in Egypt, because their sounds are the closest of all instruments to the nature of the human voice.

15

Wind Instruments

The Ancient Egyptian wind instruments can generally be classified into:

1. Instruments in which the wind vibrates in a hollow tube, like: the flute, the single pipe, ordinary pipes of the organ, etc.

2. Instruments in which a single reed causes vibration, like: clarinet, bass clarinet, reed pipes of organ, etc.

3. Instruments in which a double reed causes vibration, like the oboe and the double pipe.

4. Instruments in which elastic membranes set in vibration a column of air (lips in a mouthpiece), like: trumpet, trombone, and tuba.

Most pipes have equidistant fingerholes. The various musical scales and notes are produced by the size of the holes, the breath, the fingering, or some special device, as well as playing techniques that will be detailed in this chapter.

The Magic Nay (End-Blown Flute)

Shown is a flute from tomb near pyramids - 4th Dynasty.

Nays are made from the reed plants, which grow abundantly along the banks of the numerous irrigation canals in the Nile Valley. From this very simple plant, the Egyptians (then and now) were/are able to provide an incredible range of tones. No instrument had/has a more incorporeal sound, a sweeter *sostenuto*, a more heartfelt *vibrato*.

The Egyptian (ancient and present) *nay* differs from the present-day flute in two main ways:

1. the *nay* is made only of reed, and the flute is made of wood or metal.
2. the *nay* is end-blown, and the flute is stopped at one end and blown over a side hole.

There are also differences between the *nay* (end-blown flute) and the pipes [see page 132], regarding the length, number, and locations of fingerholes, etc.

The sounds of the Egyptian *nay* are produced by blowing through a very small aperture of the lips against the edge of the orifice of the tube, and directing the wind into the tube. By opening and closing the fingerholes, the resulting variation changes the length of air in the columns, providing the different pitches. The resulting sounds provide melodies—by steps and by leaps, brisk and longing, staccato, legato, in tender pulsations and foamy cascades.

The Egyptian *nay* (end-blown flute) changed little in appearance over the course of the Egyptian history. It is one of the most popular instruments in Egypt today.

Nays are produced in seven different lengths, between 14.8" and 26.8" (37½ and 68cm). Construction and measurement of the fingerholes of today's *nays* (end-blown flutes) still adhere to the same principles as those of Ancient Egypt, as follows:

1. They are always cut from the upper part of the reed plant.

2. Each *nay* consists of nine joints/knuckles.

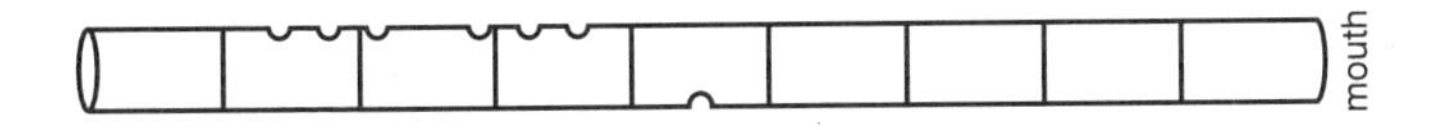

3. Each *nay* has six holes on the front, and one hole on the back. The typical layout of the finger and thumb holes are shown below:

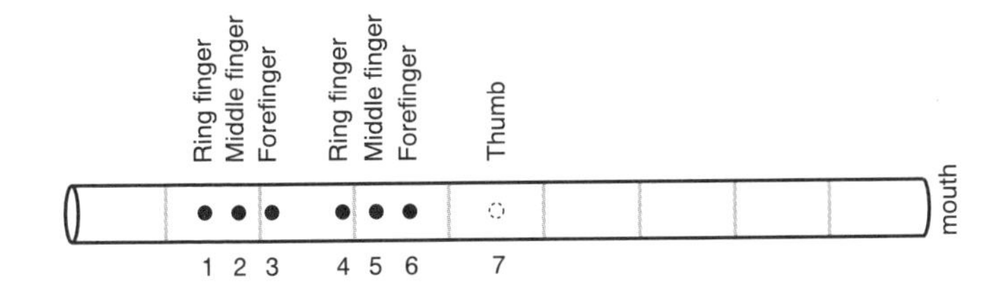

The Egyptian flute (*nay*) is considered a vertical flute. The vertical-type flutes have/had greater musical possibilities than the whistle flutes. Being able to vary the angle of blowing against the edge, the player could give more expression to the tone.

Players of the *nay* (end-blown flute) direct the instrument (to a limited extent) to the right, left, and straight ahead, as shown herein. The players were/are able to accomplish endless intermediate values, through the driving or dropping of the blowing air stream.

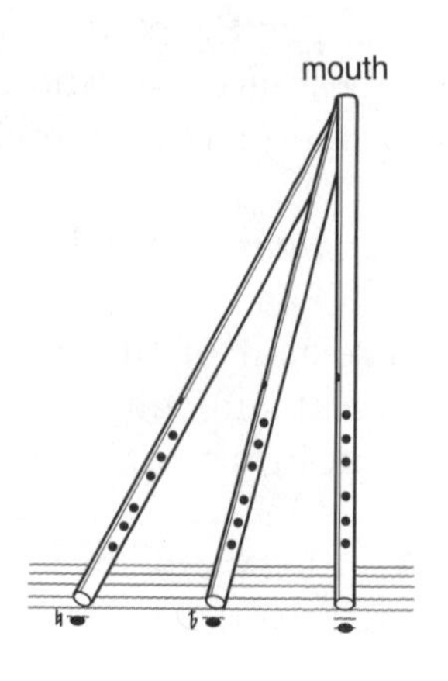

By blowing with more or less force, sounds are produced an octave higher or lower. Through the technique of over-blowing, the musician can play a range of more than three octaves.

The player requires a considerable finesse. In order to achieve any desired tone, the player must control, coordinate, and manipulate: the strength and direction of his breath; the tension of his lips; the movement of his tongue; the position of the lip and head, as well as opening or closing the fingerholes in diverse combinations.

Since a single *nay* (end-blown flute) with a certain length can only provide a limited number of musical pitches, the Egyptian musicians (then and now) used/use a set of seven different lengths of *nays*, in order to change the tonality, and/or to change the pitch through increasing or decreasing the tones. A set of seven *nays* complement each other to provide a whole and complete range of very small notes in the compass of several octaves.

The player utilized/utilizes a set of seven lengths, housed in a case, in order to obtain all tonal requirements. The seven lengths of the Egyptian *nays* (end-blown flutes) are: 26.8, 23.6, 21.3, 20.1, 17.5, 15.9, and 14.8 inches (68, 60, 54, 51, 44½, 40½, and 37½ cm).

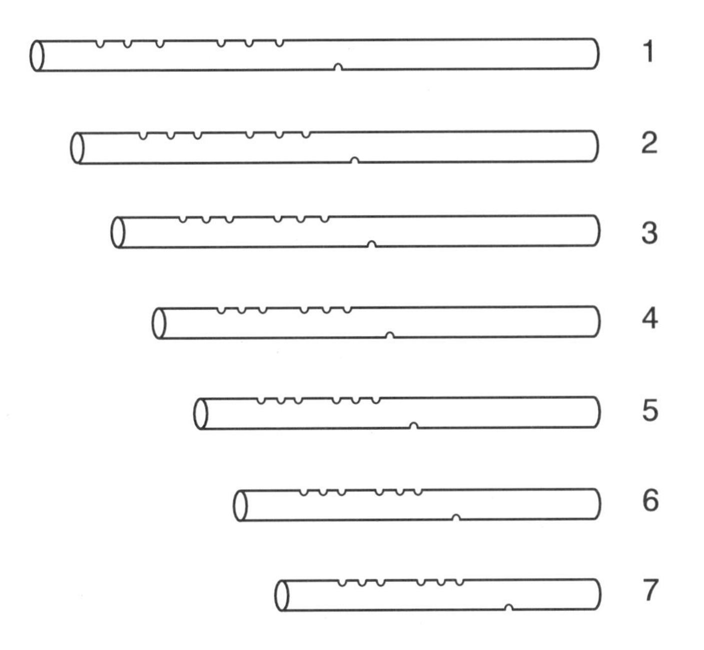

From the Middle Kingdom era [20th century BCE], Ancient Egyptian flutes from temples of Armant III give (according to C. Sachs) intervals (in cents) of 248 (11 Egyptian commas), 316 (14 commas), 182 (4 commas), with an overall range of a natural Fifth of 702 cents (31 commas).

The measurements between the examined Ancient Egyptian *nays*' fingerholes (not taking into account the various playing techniques) reveals that several tight-stepped scales were known, with intervals less than ¼ tone (equivalent to two Egyptian musical commas).

Several of these Ancient Egyptian instruments are scattered in museums and private collections throughout the world. Some examples of found and/or depicted *nays* include:

- A slate palette [ca. 3200 BCE, now at Ashmolean Museum at

Oxford] depicts a number of animals. Among them is a jackal, playing the *nay* (end-blown flute).

- Tomb of Nencheftka, Sakkara [5th Dynasty, now in the Cairo Museum] depicts a *nay* player.
- Different lengthed *nays* (end-blown flutes) from Sakkara [now in the Cairo Museum, cat. # 69815 and 69816].
- A relief from the tomb of Nekauhor at Sakkara [2390 BCE, now in the Metropolitan Museum of Art, New York].
- Representations in several tombs in **Ta-Apet** (Thebes), during the 18th Dynasty.

The Egyptian *nay* was/is important for functions related to rebirth/renewal themes [see chapters 20 and 21].

The *nay* (flute) continues to maintain its mystical significance. The most common *nay* of the modern Egyptians is known as the *Dervish nay*—because it is played by the mystical fellowship of Dervishes—to accompany the singing and dancing members, during their mystical activities.

Transverse Flute

Ancient Egyptians were familiar with transverse flutes, which were/are blown from the side, and horizontally held.

The use of the transverse flute is present in Ancient Egyptian musical scenes since the 4th Dynasty, such as the above scene from a tomb near the Giza Pyramids.

Several other representations are found in Ancient Egyptian tombs, such as an illustration of an Egyptian transverse flute player [now at the Pelizaeus Museum Hildesheim].

The Ancient Egyptian instrument had an excellent mouthpiece, which was used to evenly distribute the breath, and also functions as a wind chamber.

Some Ancient Egyptian transverse flutes made of bronze, with the above-mentioned mouthpieces, are housed in the Museum of Napoli. Other similar flutes were found in southern Egypt, towards Meroe.

Pan Flute

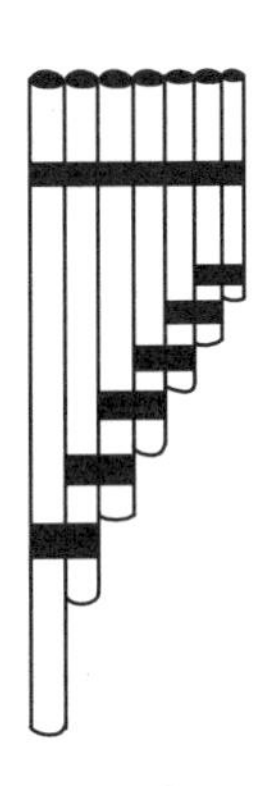

Pan-pipes, raft form

Pan-pipes were/are a set of graduated tubes, generally seven in number, each resembling a simple vertical flute. Each pipe was/is stopped at the lower end and has no fingerholes. They were all joined together to form a raft. The upper ends formed a horizontal line, so the player could shift his mouth along them according to the note required.

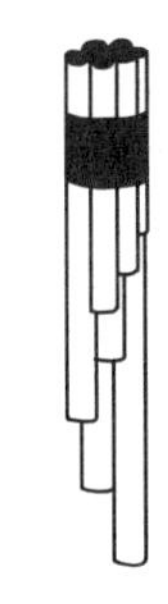

Pan-pipes, bundle form

Numerous Ancient Egyptian vessels for consecrated oil or cosmetics were found to be shaped like pan flutes. They date back to the New Kingdom, which proves that such instruments were already in existence at that time.

Relatively few instruments of that kind were excavated. A well-preserved pan flute was unearthed in a **Sobek** temple at Fayoum. Another pan flute is illustrated in *Objects of Daily Use*, by Flinders Petrie.

Single Reed Pipe (Clarinet)

Pipes of all kinds were/are made from the reed plants, which are abundant near the Egyptian irrigation canals.

The Egyptian single reed pipe (clarinet) contains a reed near the mouth that vibrates when one blows directly into the hole, through the pipe. The breath is directed through a wooden or ivory beak, onto a sharp "lip" cut in the pipe itself.

The Egyptian single reed pipe was of equal antiquity with the *nay* (flute). It was a straight tube, without any increase at the mouthpiece. The reed pipes differ from the *nay* in construction, such as length, number of holes, etc.

There are two Egyptian single reed pipes [now in the British Museum], that are 9 and 15 inches (23 and 38cm) long, and others [now in the collection at Leiden] that vary in length from 7 to 15 (18 to 38cm) inches.

Pipes had/have equidistant fingerholes. Some of the reed pipes have three holes, others four, as is the case with 14 Ancient Egyptian pipes presently at Leiden.

In order to produce a musical scale, the performer must control the size of the hole, the breath, the fingering, or by other special playing techniques.

The ratio between the fingerholes (without taking into account other playing techniques) yields the following intervals on Egyptian instruments, now at:

- the Leiden Museum [#475 and 477]—12:9:8:7:6 twelfths;
- Torino [#8] and Berlin [#20667]—12:11:10:9:8 twelfths;
- Torino [#12]—14:12:11:10:9:8:7 fourteenths;
- Torino [#11]—11:10:9:8:7: 6 elevenths.

Double Pipes

Numerous Ancient Egyptian reed pipes and double pipes were recovered from tombs and are now scattered in museums all over the world. The double pipes in Ancient Egypt had different kinds, some having only one mouthhole, and others having two, but placed so near together as to enable the performer to blow upon both pipes at the same time. The mouthpiece of a pipe consists of a thin tube, closed at the upper end. A tongue is cut into the tube, and vibrates in the player's mouth.

The pipes are either of equal length, or one is shorter than the other. They are blown simultaneously and played in unison. Sometimes, one pipe has fingerholes while the other does not. Sometimes, one pipe served as a drone accompaniment, and its holes were stopped with wax. The Egyptians occasionally inserted little pegs or tubes into some of the fingerholes, to regulate the order of intervals, or the *mode* in which they intended to perform.

As the placement of the fingerholes (and hence the tones) do not completely correspond to one another, there are certain lingering effects, as well as sharper and more penetrating tones than is the case with ordinary instruments.

This drone playing is confirmed from three facts: the peculiar arrangement of the players' fingers in Egyptian art works; the present practice in Egypt; the excavation of a pipe with all except one fingerhole stopped with wax.

Pipes with many fingerholes were used for the playing of melodies, the others for the production of an accompanying tone similar to the drone of the bagpipe. As such, the double pipe allows different playing types:

1. alternate playing,
2. octave playing,

3. a melody with a "pedal" either below or above,
4. "Duet playing", i.e. the simultaneous performance of two melodies whether rhythmically distinct or allied.

The mystical Egyptian Sufi fraternity of the Dervishes specialize in playing the double pipes.

The following is an overview of the different types of double pipes of Ancient (and present-day) Egypt:

a. **Double Clarinet** is the common name for the instrument consisting of two pipes of equal length, parallel to each other, and tied together. The pipes are made of the prolific reed plant.

Double clarinets are depicted on reliefs [from 2700 BCE], such as in the tomb of Nencheftka [5th Dynasty, Sakkara, now exhibited in Cairo Museum, cat. #11533, shown herein], which shows a double clarinet made of two canes, equal in length and identically carved. This depiction is exactly like the *zummarah*—a popular Egyptian instrument used in folk music of today. The position of fingers and the posture while playing also coincide with the modern practice of music.

playing short clarinet

The ancient (and present-day) double clarinet of Egypt is made of two canes, glued and tied alongside one another and provided with equidistant, and symmetrically arranged fingerholes (4, 5, or 6) in each cane; in the upper ends smaller canes are inserted, out of which the beating tongue is cut by a three-sided slit. The player stops the corresponding holes of both tubes simultaneously with one finger, and as the holes, roughly cut into an uneven cane, produce slightly different pitches, the effect is a pulsating sound such as in the modern occidental organ stop, *unda maris*.

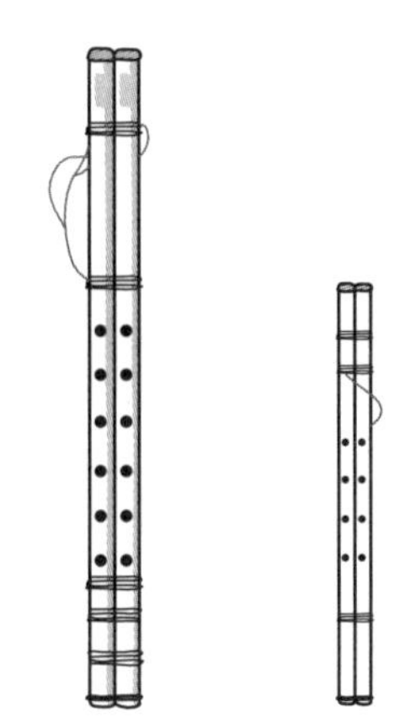

As in glass blowing, breathing is exclusively through the nose, while the mouth emits a constant blast of air. A different type of blowing is used for the modification of timbre and force, and the sound is emitted with unaltering strength and shrillness.

The Egyptian double clarinet comes in two variations, based on the style of mouthpiece:

1. the *zummarah*, which has its vibrating reed cut from the lower end of the mouthpiece. This version allows articulation of high notes, obtained by holding the instrument in a horizontal position and overblowing.

2. the *mashurah*, with the reed cut from the upper end. The instrument is held at a downwards-sloping angle, and as such, produces lower notes.

Some examples of found and/or depicted reed pipes are noted below:

- The double clarinet is depicted in Ancient Egyptian

musical scenes since the Old Kingdom (4th Dynasty), as shown on page 134.

- A double clarinet in a relief from the tomb of Nekauhor [Sakkara, 5th Dynasty, now at the Metropolitan Museum of Art, New York].

- A double clarinet player is depicted in the tomb of Imery [Giza, Old Kingdom, 5th Dynasty]. The postures, techniques of playing, as well as the number of the fingerholes are shown. One of these holes is seen at the forefinger of the widely stretched right hand of the player.

- A 12" (31cm) long double clarinet from the New Kingdom era [now at the Cairo Museum, cat. #69837 and 69838].

b. Double Oboe is the common name for the instrument consisting of two reed pipes of equal length in divergent positions. Each pipe has a reed that causes vibrations. The result is a type of polyphony with heterphonic expression.

There are many depictions in Ancient Egyptian tombs, detailing this instrument. Some show the
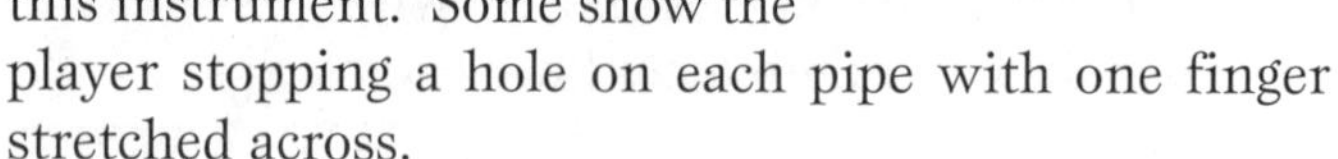
player stopping a hole on each pipe with one finger stretched across.

Surviving oboes, since the Old Kingdom, were found in cases, each containing a set of different lengths—from 8 to 24 inches (20-60cm). The number of holes ranges from 3 to 7 to 11.

Today's players of oboes, like their ancestors, also possess several instruments, which are put together as a set in a case, in order to satisfy all tonal requirements of their repertoire.

Some examples of found and/or depicted oboes include:

- A quiver-formed case, discovered near Dier el-Bakhit [tomb no. 37, Ta-Apet (Thebes), New Kingdom, now at the Cairo Museum, cat #69836], comprised six oboe pipes (three double oboes). The found case contained fragments of the mouthpiece—oboe "sheets" made of straw.
  In order to meet all tonal requirements of the performances, the player placed small wax lumps in the unneeded fingerholes. Several fingerholes of these oboes still contain this filling, and even a piece of wax was found in a case.

- A double oboe [shown herein] is depicted in the tomb of Nakht [Ta-Apet (Thebes), dated from the 15th century BCE]. The instrument has several fingerholes—some visible, others are covered by the musician's hands.

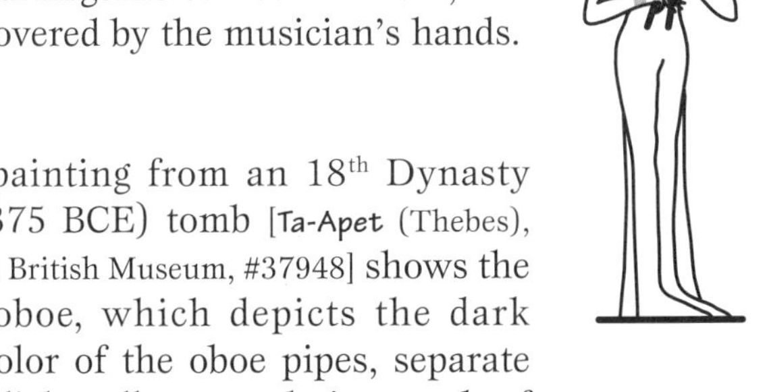

- A wall painting from an 18th Dynasty (1425-1375 BCE) tomb [Ta-Apet (Thebes), now at the British Museum, #37948] shows the double oboe, which depicts the dark brown color of the oboe pipes, separate from the light yellow mouthpiece made of straw.
  In effect, oboes used to be blown with straw "sheets", as shown by excavated instruments.

c. **Arghool** is the name of the instrument consisting of a double clarinet with pipes of different lengths, parallel to each other and laced together. One pipe is much longer than the other. The longer pipe serves as a drone, providing a prolonged organ point. The shorter pipe provides the melody type.

One of the reed pipes of the *arghool* contains no fingerholes at all, or a number remarkably less than the melody reed.

The bourdon pipes are some yards/meters long, and can, according to the player's discretion, be elongated by mostly two extensions, in order to turn from one mode to another. Adjectival extensions determine the size of the instrument (small, middle-sized, or huge instruments), as well as the number of fingerholes (five, six, or seven).

As with the case of the double clarinet, there are two versions of *arghool* mouthpieces: the *zummarah* and the *mashurah* [see details of both on page 135].

d. **Others**

The principle and method of playing the double pipes applies also to the bagpipe, where its prototypes date back to Ancient Egypt.

Ancient Egyptians have also developed and used the organ (in its pneumatic and hydraulic form).

The Twin Horns/Trumpets

Horns/trumpets were known in Ancient Egypt since its very early times.

Generally, trumpets in Ancient Egypt always appeared in pairs. With the typical two horns: one was sounded at dawn, the other at dusk.

Buq/buk is an Egyptian (not Arabic) word that means *mouth*. It was out of the divine mouth (**Ra**) that the divine sound (**Tehuti**) came, with the harmonic series (over- and under-tone series).

The more or less conical horn *(al-buq)* has survived in the Spanish terms: *alboque, alboquea,* or *albuquea*.

The Egyptian trumpet was straight, like the later Roman tuba, or the present-day trumpet. Ancient Egypt had a variety of trumpets. They were generally 2 to 3 feet (60-90cm) long, and made of brass or bronze, with mouthpieces, and with flares or "bells" at the other end.

The horn/trumpet was not a "military" instrument. The sounds of the horns/trumpets were related to rebirth motifs—a transition from one stage to another. As such, they were/are utilized:

- Then and now, during funerary processions to "wake up" the deceased (resurrection). As such, it was attributed to **Ausar** (Osiris), the principle of resurrection.

- To mark/announce both the new day (at dusk) and the end of the night (at dawn). Two different horns for two different but complementary purposes. They were both used in temple rituals.

- To celebrate rebirth, as in the New Year celebration.

Some found and depicted trumpets include:

- A trumpet player in the Kagemni tomb [ca. 2300 BCE, Sakkara].

- A wall painting from the tomb of Nebamon [Ta-Apet (Thebes), Tomb 90, ca. 1410 BCE] shows a trumpet player, who precedes a funeral procession.

- Silver and golden (maybe copper) trumpets, from the tomb of Tut-Ankh-Amen [1361-1352 BCE, now at the Cairo Museum, cat. #69850 and 69851]. The trumpets [shown herein] were found separate from one another. The silver trumpet measured 22.5" (57.1 cm), while the copper one was only 19.5" (49.5 cm) in length. Both ended with flares or "bells". The ratio between the lengths of the two trumpets is 8:9—the Perfect Tone.

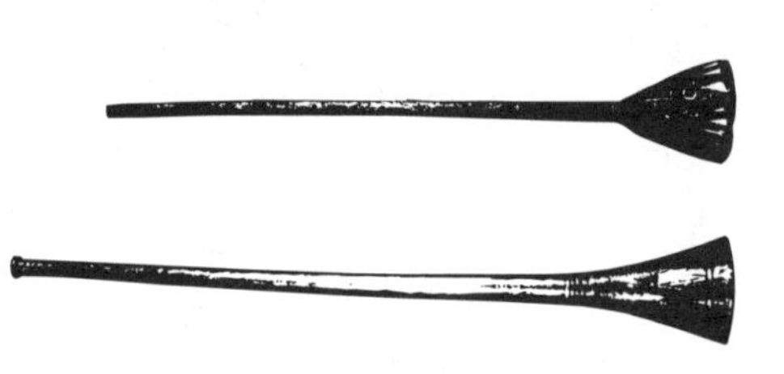

- A trumpet blower of the Apet (New Year) procession is depicted in a relief from the temple of Luxor, from the time of Tut-Ankh-Amen [1361-1352 BCE].

16

Percussion Instruments

Percussion instruments can be categorized under membrano- and non-membrano-phone instruments, i.e. whether or not a skin or parchment-type sheet is used.

Membrano-Phone Instruments

a. Drums

Ancient Egypt had a wealth and variety of drums of different shapes, sizes, and functions. Some with skin on one or both sides. Some were struck with sticks, others with fingers and palms.

We are acquainted with three main kinds of the Ancient Egyptian drum.

1. **Cylindrical**. This kind of drum does not appear in any of the walls of tombs or temples (evidence that the variety of Ancient Egyptian instruments is not limited to the depicted musical scenes in the tombs and temples).

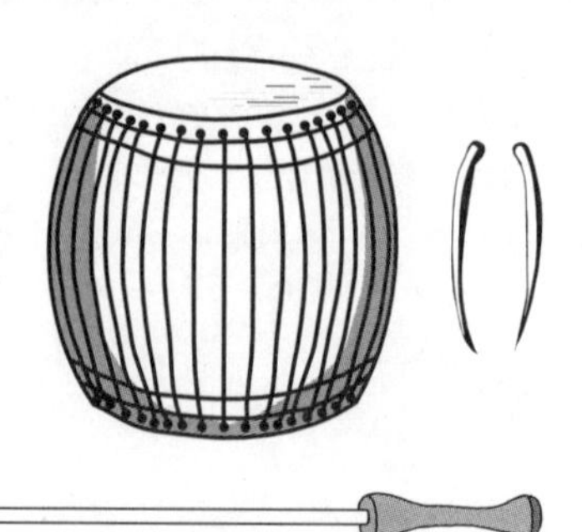

A few actual drums were found in the Ancient Egyptian tombs. A drum [shown herein, now at the Berlin Museum] is 1½ ft. (46cm) high, and 2 ft. (61cm) broad. Like other similar drums, it had cords for bracing it, and the cords could be tightened or slackened.

It was beaten with two drumsticks slightly bent. The Egyptians also had straight drumsticks with a handle, and a knob at the end. Some of these are now in the Berlin Museum.

2. **Small hand drum**—elongated barrel-shape from 2 to 3 feet (61-91cm) in length, covered with parchment at both ends. The performer was able to beat with his hands, fingers, or knuckles on both ends.

3. **Single skin drum**, which is a smaller type. This type was also rarely depicted in tombs. There are two kinds of this drum. The first kind is the earthen *tabla/darabukkah* (also called *goblet drum*). It is usually from 1½ ft. to 2 ft. (46cm to 61cm) long. The other kind is made of wood, inlaid with mother-of-pearl and tortoise-shell, covered with a piece of fish's skin at the larger extremity, open at the smaller end, and about 15 inches (38cm) in length.

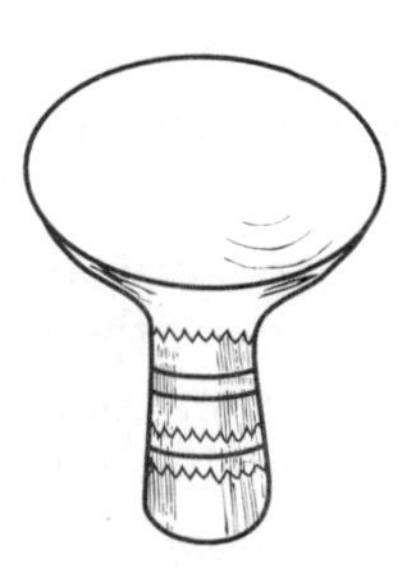

The membrane is struck with both hands. Drum playing with the bare hands, knuckles, and fingers has, in Egypt, reached perfection in technique, variety of timbre, and intricacy of rhythm. A good *tabla/darabukkah* player, like a tambourine player, must have a command of the entire rhythmic patterns (timing—setting the tempo) repertoire.

The player produces the heavy principal beats, as with the frame drum, at the center, whereas the light secondary beats are produced near the rim. Differentiating the sounds in this way, the drum player is able to present the rhythmic timing.

b. Tambourines

The *tambourine* (*riqq/tar*) is a single-headed instrument with a diameter of approximately 8" (20 cm), covered with fish skin, or with a goatskin membrane. The frame is mounted with ten pairs of cymbals set inside vertical pairs of "cymbal windows" that are cut out of the frame in a symmetrical arrangement. The tambourine is held in the left hand by the thumb and the fingers in such a manner that the fingers can also strike the rim of the frame. The right hand maneuvers at the center as well as at the edge of the membrane. These two positions correspond to a light drum beat and a heavy one, and as such, they set the required rhythmic timing.

The *daff* (*duff*), like the *riqq/tar*, is a tambourine. This instrument, however, has a larger diameter—approximately 12" (30 cm)—and a shallower frame. It is not used to perform rhythmic timing (*wazn*) patterns.

Examples of Ancient Egyptian membrano-phone instruments include:

- A fragment from Ne-user-re's temple of the Sun, near Abusir [ca. 2700 BCE, now in the Munich museum], shows the top of a large drum.

- A 4,000 year old cylindrical drum [now in the Cairo Museum] was found in good condition in a tomb in Beni Hassan. It is 25.6 inches (65 cm) long and 11.4 inches (29 cm) wide, and has a network of thongs with a tightening tourniquet to stretch the leather skins. Both eardrums were strongly tightened together in a crosswise position, which pulled them firmly to one another.

- A number of drummers accompany the **Apet** Festival procession, depicted in the Luxor Temple, from the time of Tut-Ankh-Amen [1361-1352 BCE].

- A well preserved drum [dated from the 18th Dynasty, now at the Cairo Museum cat. #69355] has the same dimensions as the drum from Beni Hassan's tomb [see above], but the body of the drum is made of bronze.

- A squared drum is depicted on a wall painting in the tomb of Rekhmire [from **Ta-Apet** (Thebes), Tomb 100, dated to the first half of the 15th century BCE].

- There are several other drums in many museums throughout the world [such as the Metropolitan Museum of Art in New York and the Louvre in Paris], which are tightened in the same manner as the one mentioned above at the Cairo Museum.

- Small frame drums (*riqq/tar*) of the New Kingdom were found. Most of them were circular, but some had four concave sides.

- Some specimens of Egyptian circular frame drums can be seen in more than one museum.

Non-Membrano-Phone (Idiophone) Instruments

a. Percussion Sticks

Percussion sticks are considered to be a type of clapper. They have been recorded on Ancient Egyptian vases made before 3000 BCE, carefully drawn. Percussion sticks consist of two sticks, each held in a hand or both held in one hand and clapped against one another by the players.

Scenes of playing with percussion sticks are depicted in Ancient Egyptian tombs, as a part of ritual dances during times of harvest. In an Ancient Egyptian tomb of about 2700 BCE, a representation of a file of farmers are shown clapping sticks together, as they advance in those long, easy strides typical of fertility rites in a ritual dance.

Similar presentations are found in other tombs of the Old Kingdom, such as a relief from the tomb of Neferirtenef, Sakkara [now in the Royal Museums of Art and of History, in Brussels].

Percussion sticks were also played during the pressing of grapes, as depicted in several tombs. Currently we know of four similar scenes. In each of them, we have two musicians who kneel opposite to one another, surrounded by an oval-shaped outline, each holding two pieces of wood in their hands. A clear example is depicted on a wall relief from the tomb of Mereruka (Sakkara, Old Kingdom). While the vintners press the grapes with their feet, two other men are clapping the rhythm with their sticks, one held in each hand. [See page 157 for an illustration and more info.]

b. Clappers

The Ancient Egyptian clappers were used in all types of occasions. Clappers were/are frequently used to regulate the music and the dance. They varied slightly in form. Some were made of wood, bone, ivory, or shells, others of brass (or some sonorous metal). Some have a straight handle, surmounted by a head or other ornamental device. Sometimes the handle is slightly curved, and double, with two heads at the upper extremity. Clappers' heads were carved in the shape of animal presentations, falcon heads, bearded men, lotus flowers, gazelles, cow heads. Many are decorated with the head of **Het-Heru** (Hathor).

Hundreds of such clappers were found in Ancient Egyptian tombs.

The performer held a clapper in each hand, and the sound depended on their size and material of which they were made.

Sample representations include:

- Ivory clappers, from the 1st or 2nd Dynasty [now in the Cairo Museum, cat. #69457 and 69250].

- A pair of ivory clappers shaped like human hands, dating back to the 18th Dynasty [now in the Metropolitan Museum in New York].

- Two ivory clappers [now in the Cairo Museum, cat. #69234 and 69235].

- Straight ivory clappers in hand form [now in the Cairo Museum, cat. #69206].

c. Sistrums/Sistra

The Ancient Egyptian sistrum was the sacred instrument *par excellence*, and belonged to the service of the temple.

It generally had 3 to 4 bars, and the whole instrument was from 8 to 16 or 18 inches (20, 40, 47cm) in length, entirely of brass or bronze. It was sometimes inlaid with silver, or gilt, or otherwise ornamented. It was held upright and shaken, the rings moving to and fro upon the bars. The sistrum's bars were frequently made to imitate the asp, or were simply bent at each end to secure them.

It was so great a privilege to hold the sacred sistrum in the temple, that it was given to queens, and to those noble ladies who had the distinguished title of *Women of* ***Amun***, and were devoted to the service of the deity.

Numerous representations of sistra were depicted throughout Egypt's dynastic history. A large number of Ancient Egyptian sistra were found, and are now in museums throughout the world.

d. Cymbals

The Egyptian cymbals were made of brass, or of silver and brass mixed. They varied in diameter from 5½ to 7 inches (14-18cm), and were shaped just like modern instruments, even to the saucer-like depression in the middle.

Numerous cymbals were found buried in Ancient Egyptian tombs, and are now scattered in museums throughout the world. The specimens preserved [in the Metropolitan Museum of Art in New York] are of two different sizes: 5 and 7 inches (12 and 18cm) in diameter.

e. Castanets

Tiny fingertip pairs of cymbals also were in use in Ancient Egypt. In later ages, these were carried by the Moors to Spain where they became known as *castanets* because they were made of chestnut (castaña).

These small-type cymbals, 2" to 3" (5-7.5 cm) in diameter, are played between thumb and middle finger up to this day. Castanets—called *crotala*—are used in pairs, and are struck together while dancing. The term *castanets* is used here in the narrower sense of clappers, the striking faces of which are hollowed out to give a fuller resonance.

Egyptian castanets existed in two forms: 1) shaped something like a very small wooden boot, cut in half, lengthwise, and grooved in the leg part, while the tapering foot part served as a handle; 2) nearly the shape of modern Spanish *castañuelas*, but it was less flat and looked like the chestnut, *castaña*, for which it was named.

Numerous Egyptian castanets were found in Ancient Egyptian tombs, and are now scattered throughout the museums and private collections worldwide.

The religious significance of castanets is shown in the musical scene of four musicians with castanets, depicted in the **Apet** procession at the Luxor Temple, from the time of Tut-Ankh-Amen [ca. 1360 BCE].

f. Bells (Chimes)

Ancient Egyptian bells of various kinds were found carefully wrapped in cloth, before they were placed in the tombs. A large number of these bells are now housed at the Egyptian Museum of Cairo. The sounds of some of them were tested, and it was proven that they have quite an extensive range of sound and tone pitches. They varied in weight, in order to provide the various musical ratios of 9:8 for a whole note, 3:2 for the Fifth, and so on.

Bells were made mainly of bronze, but were also occasionally made of gold or silver. They came in different forms. Some have the form of bells with a jagged mouth, which is to represent a flower calyx—among a whole line of other types.

Having a large number of Ancient Egyptian bell molds [now in the Cairo Museum, cat. #32315a, b] provides good evidence of the metal founding in Ancient Egypt. The influx hole for the liquid metal can be clearly seen.

The chemical analysis of the typical Ancient Egyptian bell was found to be 82.4% copper, 16.4% tin, and 1.2% lead.

Bells had/have a religious and functional significance in Egypt. Bells were worn by the temple priests during the temple rituals. Bells were also used in the Ancient Egyptian festivals related to **Ausar** (Osiris).

Bells are utilized as amulets, to protect people against evil spirits. Bells are suspended at the door to be rung by entering persons—not to warn the owner of their arrival—but to protect the house and the caller against the demons who lurk under the threshold.

Some other representations of Ancient Egyptian bells include:

- Animals with bells on a pre-dynastic vase, Negadah I Period.

- Fifteen bells are now present in the British Museum.

- Small bells from the New Kingdom era [now in the Cairo Museum, cat. #69594].

- Scenes of the inner part of the temple of **Het-Heru** (Hathor) in Dendera, depict the priests wearing pieces of jewelry formed as bells, attached to their outfits, at their foot bangles or at their sandals. Again, the true sense is that the little bell is an amulet, whose function is to avert evil forces, which protects the priests in the presence of deities.

- Many Ancient Egyptian necklaces of gold and silver consist of bell shapes, as shown in several museums.

g. Xylophone and Glockenspiel

An Egyptian instrument is represented as a companion to the lyre, in an Ancient Egyptian tomb. The instrument consists of a series of metallic bars, or of wooden slabs, arranged according to a certain order of intervals. It appears to be a kind of dulcimer. Or, even more likely, it may be a harmonicon.

Human Parts (hands, fingers, thighs, feet, etc)

The Egyptian clapping with hands and stamping with feet has turned at an early time into a finely graded, dynamic and varied means of expression, and thus acquired an additional significance in Egypt where it turned into a high art in their culture of music.

Rhythmic clapping of two groups of men and women from the tomb of Dhutmos (Tomb 342), Ta-Apet (Thebes) [18th Dynasty, now in the British Museum]

Egyptian clapping, footstamping, and finger snapping consisted of rhythmic beats, whether simple or complicated rhythms, tonally nuanced, and dynamically well balanced. The tonal differences were produced in such a manner, that clapping used to take place as in Spain with *palmas sordas* or with *palmas brillantes*, i.e. with hollow or flat hands. In addition, and since primeval times, all possible other forms of body beats existed.

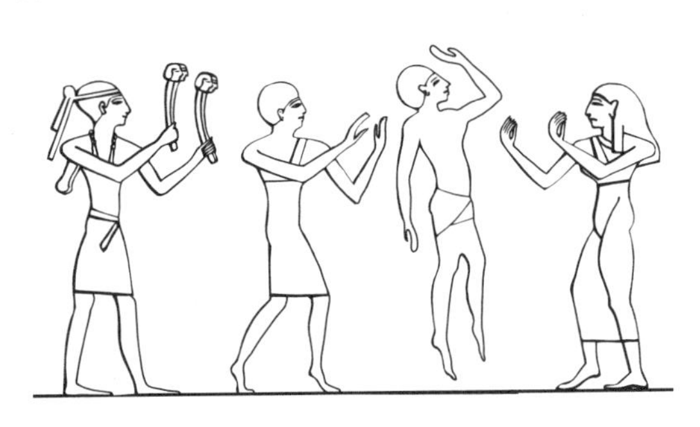

Hand-clapping of two groups [as shown above] can be between men and women or two groups of men or two groups of women. Two rhythmic accompanying patterns are played (say 12 beats and 8 beats for the first and second groups). The hand-clapping marks the fundamental rhythmic beats until a rhythmic structure of a particular density is created by the interplay of the clapping patterns performed by the two groups.

Two groups of women are shown in rhythmic hand-clapping in the **Sed** Festival, tomb of Kheruef, **Ta-Apet** (Thebes), 18th Dynasty (15th century BCE).

This form of musical production was considered heavenly in nature. One finds the passage (§§1972, 1975b) of the **Unas Transformational** (so-called *Pyramid*) **Texts** that dates to around 2350 BCE. The passage describes the muses celebrating the successful resurrection and arrival of Unas (24th century BCE) to a higher realm.

> *The double doors of heaven are open....The Souls of Buto dance for thee, they clap their hands for thee, they let loose their hair for thee, they beat their thigh for thee. They say to thee, Osiris N: 'Thou art gone, thou art come, thou sleepest, thou art awake, thou landest, thou livest.'*

Part

Maintaining the Heavenly Rhythms

17

The Universal Harmony

The Universal Musical Balance

As stated earlier, the Ancient Egyptians believed that the creation of the world was an orderly event that came as a result of the soundwaves caused by the Big Bang. The order of the created world is maintained by the principle of cosmic order, balance, and equilibrium—**Ma-at**.

Maintaining harmony in the universe requires that the world in whole and parts, are all in tune. Therefore, the sound that man creates in music, singing, or dancing (vibrating body), can either strengthen or imperil the equilibrium of the world. As such, correctness in sound generation, for the Ancient Egyptians, was/is essential to the cosmos, as well as the welfare of the individual and the society.

In Ancient Egypt, the proper coordination of sound production (words, song, music, and dances)—between earth and the heavens—was clearly acknowledged and appreciated in Plato's collected dialogues, such as *Laws II* [656c-657c] [see pages 78-79 of this book], as well as in *Laws VII* [798e–799b], as shown herein:

ATHENIAN: Every means, then, shall ***we say, must be employed to keep our children from the desire to reproduce different models in dance or song****, as well as to prevent a possible tempter from offering them the inducement of a variety of delights ?*
CLINIAS: Perfectly true.

ATHENIAN: Well, ***can any of us find a better device for this purpose than that employed in Egypt?***
CLINIAS: And what is that?
ATHENIAN: Why, ***the plan is to consecrate all our dances and all our tunes****. First, the festivals must be fixed by compiling an annual calendar to show what feasts are to be celebrated, at what dates, and in honor of what deities, sons of deities, or spirits, respectively.*

Next, ***certain authorities must determine what hymn is to be sung on the feast of each divinity, and by what dances the ceremony of the day is to be graced****. When this has been determined, the whole citizen body must do public sacrifice to the Destinies and the entire pantheon at large, and consecrate each hymn to its respective god or other patron by solemn libation. If any man tries to introduce hymn or dance into the worship of any deity in contravention of these canons, the priests of either sex, acting in conjunction with the curators of law, shall have the warrant both of religion and law in excluding him from the festival;*

The highlights of the above statements are:

1. Music, singing, and dancing must be performed/selected according to a well thought out selection of melodies that are appropriate for the different occasions.

2. The Egyptians have had established melodies for all kinds of occasions.

3. Egypt was the ideal model for such rules.

The Theme of Balanced Polarity

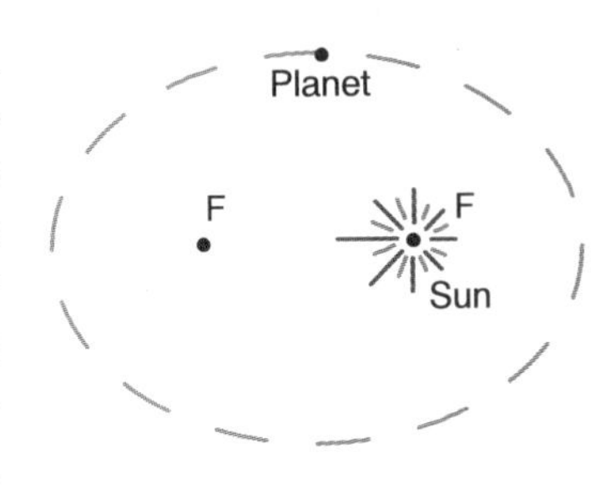

Maintaining the universal musical balance meant conforming to the natural cosmic law of balanced polarity. As stated earlier, each planetary system is balanced only when the planet's orbit is an egg-shaped plane that has two foci, with its sun's center of mass at one of its foci. Similarly, the Egyptian traditions—including music and dance—follow the same pattern.

We noted earlier that the diatonic scale has two energy centers [see chapter 2]. Balanced polarity in musical terms is represented through the alternate action between two different and complementary energies (like inhaling–exhaling).

The concept of this musical form is represented in a typical Ancient Egyptian musical scene since the Old Kingdom (4500 years ago). An example can be found in the walls of Mereruka's tomb [6th Dynasty, Sakkara], which shows two men squatting inside an egg-shaped oval, beating two percussion sticks together. The scene represents the typical Egyptian **dor**, a piece of music with a refrain. Other similar graphical representations are depicted in Ancient Egyptian tombs, in the grape harvest scenes, as well as harvest scenes of men dancing while the grain is being taken to the granary.

The application of balanced polarity—alternating sounds—applies to all types of musical performances in Ancient and present-day Egypt, as follows:

1. By musical instruments—in several varieties, such as:

- **a.** by two different instruments.
- **b.** by one single instrument, such as a double clarinet, double oboe—whereby one pipe is used for the melody and a second for the bourdon.
  Or by a string instrument (harp, lyre or lute), on which a deep string is always stricken—in order to support the melody produced by the same instrument; or by another player or by a singer.
- **c.** between a single (or group of) instrument(s) and the rest of the orchestra.

[See chapters 14 and 15 for additional related information.]

2. Alternate singing, the archetype of responsorial and antiphonal practice of singing, was the specialty of the Egyptians since ancient times. Present *Baladi* Egyptians of rural population continue the very same tradition—where their singing form, structure, and pattern are rendered by a choir leader (a leading voice). The lead singer provides the melismatic solo parts, and was/is usually accompanied by 4-6 singers who perform the rhythmically formal, strongly bound refrain-like sections.

Alternating singing may also occur between male and female individuals or male and female groups.

3. Singing and instruments alternating between a singer and a musical instrument (or instruments).

4. Dances were/are also performed on the alternating sound principle, i.e. the energy generated from/by two focal points in the round-shaped formation of dancers or participants. [More about "circle" dance in chapters 19, 20, and 21.]

The Dor-ian Musical Suites

The Egyptian musical compositions are organized in a series form—to correspond to the pulsations of the cosmic nature. The Egyptian **Dor** is a musical series composed of several well coordinated melodic passages that are split up by well determined pauses. The suite goes from one musical mode (known in Arabic as *maqam*) to another, in a series, with specific emphasis and flow from one to the other. Each passage of a **Dor** has its own peculiar emotional content. As such, each passage had/has its own peculiar tones selection and arrangement around its structured nuclei with its distinct meter and regular structure. Each passage's component fits in the overall content of the completed series—**Dor**. [Details of musical formulations of modes is found in chapter 11.]

The Ancient Egyptian practice of the **Dor-ian** musical suite found its way to Europe. It is interesting to note that the musical term, *suite*, according to the *Oxford Companion to Music*, means *a musical series.* It was called in ancient French, *ordre*, in German, *partita or partie*, and in Italian, *sonata da camera*. During the 17th and 18th centuries, the English term for it was *lesson*. It is usually composed of 4 to 12 or more consecutive musical pieces. Examples of such suites are *The Nutcracker*, *Swan Lake*, etc.

However, in Ancient and *Baladi* Egypt, the choice of musical composition and related singing and dancing conformed to intentionally designed patterns, as is noted throughout the text of this book.

18

The Vocal Powers

Generating Sounds

The most basic of all musical instruments is the human voice. The human voice was/is the instrument *par excellence* of the priest and the enchanter in Ancient Egypt.

The typical gesture of the Egyptian singer has always been, since ancient times, to put one or both his hands to his ear(s), to control/regulate the pitch of his singing. This gesture serves the fortification of sound, because the singer may hear his voice louder and stronger, and even slightly changed.

We repeatedly see this posture in the reliefs and wall paintings of the Old and New Kingdoms. A powerful example is found in a wall relief from the tomb of Patenemhab [Sakkara, 18th Dynasty, now in the Leiden Museum]. One can recognize the blind harpist's head resonance while singing, by observing the muscle contractions of the forehead and steep muscle contractions on the bridge of the nose and both sides of the mouth—indicating nasal singing from a compressed throat at a high pitch. The queer nasaling is caused by a tiny membrane that screens the voice and colors it in covibration.

The Egyptian (Ancient and present-day Sufi) singer was/is well trained to generate the widest compass, variation and articulation of sounds, by utilizing the four agents that cooperate in producing the needed tones, particular sections on pitch, loudness, and timbre. They are:

1. **Wind Supply.** This is accomplished by the proper breathing techniques. The breathing cycle, in-out-rest, tension-relaxation-balance, are all critical to the success of the music. Breathing lies at the root of rhythm and phrasing.

2. **Tone Producer.** The vocal cords are the actual tone producer. They are a pair of muscles in the larynx that set up the primary vibration. The vibration is started by an air stream sent against them from the lungs.

3. **Amplifiers.** The bones and cavities throughout the head and the upper part of the body participate in resonating the sound—to provide amplification.
Accordingly, one speaks of a head tone and a chest tone. Head resonance favors the high overtones. Chest resonance favors the lower overtones. The correct ratio of these two main resonators, to each other, accounts for a clear, bright, and free tone. Both adjust to each other all the time, and function simultaneously.

4. **Articulators.** Articulation of the sound is accomplished by the activity of the mouth and all its components.

Vocal Music Themes

In chapter 6, we showed how the Egyptians perceived language and music as two sides of the same coin. Each letter has its own musical form—with its particular energy. Words and phrases must be composed in the same manner as musical compositions—by the careful threading of selected notes/letters.

Patterns of set rhythms or lengths of phrases of Ancient Egyptian poems, praises, hymns, and songs of all kinds, which are known to have been chanted or performed with some musical accompaniment, were rhythmic with uniform meters and a structured rhyme.

Ancient Egyptian texts show that Egyptians spoke and sang in musical patterns on all occasions and for all purposes—from the most sacred to the most mundane. Present-day Egyptians are like their ancestors—they love to sing about anything and everything. There is nothing that is too insignificant or too large to sing a song to (or about).

All the Ancient Egyptian songs and dances are part of the function/process of each activity. The treasure of songs included simple workers' calls or extended songs, performed in all types of occupations, such as: farmers, fishermen and artisans. All various occasions had their appropriate songs, such as: lamentations and songs to the deceased; hymns, litanies and entertainment songs of philosophical content; love songs; festive songs during the Nile floods; the Egyptian New Year celebration; sung and recited prayers or spells in honor of the **neteru** (gods); songs to welcome the morning sun, etc. Several other types of songs and dances will be shown in the next chapters.

Each type of song had/has its appropriate mode/melody to suit the occasion, either of rejoicing and festivity, of solemnity, or of lamentation.

As noted on pages 80-81, spoken, written, and musical composition follow the same exact patterns. All types of vocal music themes were/are composed based on **Tehuti's** number—eight—the rhythmic number in the universe. The normal vocal musical sentence is that of eight measures, frequently (but not necessarily) divided into two half sentences of four measures each. That is, after four or eight bars of the music you will instinctively expect and will usually get a rhythmic cadence.

Just like musical compositions, there are sentences or phrases that are shorter and longer than four or eight phrases; these are brought about by omissions, overlappings, extensions, repetitions, or expansions.

Consistent with **Tehuti's** (Thoth) number being eight, there are eight types of graduated vocal music—from the pure non-musical word (plain talking)—to the pure music, which Egyptians (Ancient and Sufi) master. The shades graduated from monotone—recitative, chant, and ultimately pure musical vocalization—with no literary context.

Some forms of the Egyptian vocal music themes were/are:

1. **Poetry:** Both poetry and singing followed similar rules for musical composition. Poetry is written not only with a rhyme scheme, but also with a recurring pattern of accented and unaccented syllables. Each syllable alternates between accented and unaccented, making a double/quadruple meter and several other varieties.

2. **Recitative:** This is the typical Egyptian format/mode for learning everything, since ancient times. This form of musical poetry makes it easy to learn, memorize, and recall volumes of information of all types—astronomy, astrology, medical diagnoses and remedies, folkloric traditions, ...etc., for Ancient and *Baladi* Egyptians.

3. **Chanting**: Given the importance of chants, spells, and a person's name in Ancient Egypt, it is clear that the sound of the words must have had a functional connection with their meanings. For them, speaking was a process of generating sonar fields, establishing an immediate vibratory identity with the essential principle that underlies any object or form. Chanting in the prescribed rhythm(s) was important during temple rituals, medical procedures and administration of medicine, as well as for the deceased's funerary rites [read more about these applications in chapter 21].

4. **Musical Vocalization** is called *Layali*. Such vocalization is a must in any Egyptian musical composition. The singer utilizes the syllables of three words (*ya, leal-y,* and *ein-y*), to generate musical notes, by using his vocal capacity—as detailed earlier in this chapter. There is no match in the world for the descendants of the Ancient Egyptians—the Sufi singers—in articulating a musical composition with pitches, loudness, timbre, color, compass, ...etc., by using the four components of their vocal powers.

19

Rhythmic Dancing

The Lord of the [Song and] Dance

The significant role and impact of dance (as well as music) in Ancient Egypt was clearly acknowledged and appreciated by Plato, in *Laws VII* [798e–799b] [see text on page 156]. Here are the sentences related to dance only:

> *The plan is to consecrate all our dances. . . .*
> *. . . Certain authorities must determine what hymn is to be sung on the feast of each divinity, and by what dances the ceremony of the day is to be graced.*

Dancing is movement of various degrees (slow to fast). Movements cause vibrations that in turn produce sounds. We don't hear all soundwaves (resulting from these vibrations), but we are affected by them, nevertheless. The vibrating (dancing) body produces sound—kinetic intermittence at regular intervals—just like the musical tones produced by a vibrating string of an instrument.

Dances and songs were performed by the Pharaoh himself—as part of the temple rituals. The Pharaoh was, as such, the *Lord of the [Song and] Dance*.

In the Hall of Offerings, at Dendera Temple, a song celebrating the taming of the lioness, goes:

> ***The Pharaoh comes, to dance.***
> ***He comes, to sing.***
> ***Mistress, look, how he dances!***
> ***Het-Heru** [Hathor], **look, how he jumps!***

The **netert** (goddess) **Het-Heru** (Hathor) herself was lovingly referred to as the *Mistress of Dance* and the *Mistress of Music*. **Ausar** (Osiris) was also referred to as *"...fond of music and dance"* [read more on page 173].

Dancing is much more than sensation and pleasure. It is life and unity with nature. The proper rhythm of the dance elevates the dancer to a higher realm. His/her body becomes a medium which, through connecting to the ancestors, becomes the bearer of all the forces of nature. The dancer, possessed by his deified ancestor, is being transformed into this spirit, and is drawn into the circle of those supernatural forces in charge of the operation of fertility, victory, and the course of the stars.

The Ancient Egyptian temples maintained dancers of both sexes as a special class. We find them over and over again, either in the quiet dance, with gentle steps and with arms outstretched in rhomboid form, or in the most daring acrobatic positions.

The Ancient Egyptians combined music (and sometimes singing) with their dancing rituals. Because of its significance, the Ancient and *Baladi* Egyptians had/have schools and instructors to teach ritualistic dances (and songs) for practically all their affairs. [Samples of activities that include dancing are shown in this and subsequent chapters.]

Dancing Types

The walls of the Ancient Egyptian tombs and temples depict a wide variety of dancing styles, forms, and purposes—each for a certain time and place.

The energy level for the different types varied from the slow/gesture dance, to acrobatic, to dances out of harmony with the body—either as pure or weakened convulsive dances, to the most frenzied exhausting dances. Except for the latter, they were all choreographed.

There is a common fallacy that in the days of the Old Kingdom, Egyptian dance was slow and simple, while in the New Kingdom, steps became rounded and gliding. This is not true, because there were quiet dances in the New Kingdom and excited dancing steps in the Old Kingdom. There was/is a time, place, and purpose for each type.

The following is a very short overview of some of the Ancient and *Baladi* Egyptian dance themes:

1. Slow.

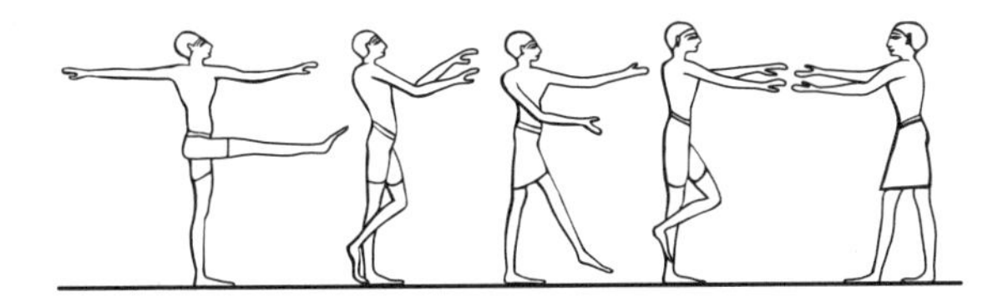

Slow and gesture dances are found in Ancient Egyptian tombs, since the Old Kingdom. These ritual dance movements are curiously similar to those practiced today in certain groups devoted to "inner development".

2. **Belly Dancing.** Belly dancing is falsely perceived as sheer sensational entertainment. In its original Egyptian form, it was a ritualistic and thoughtful dance—just like a flamenco dance. An example of this type of dancing can be found in a wall painting from the Nebaman tomb at Ta-Apet (Thebes) [shown herein], 18th Dynasty (1425-1375) [now in the British Museum *(No. 37948)*].

3. **Ballet.** On the wall scenes of tombs dating around 1800 BCE, Egyptians are shown performing pirouettes forward and backward, cartwheels, splits, and backward flips. They would do pirouettes in different positions—head up and head down alternately. Depictions of ballet scenes are found in tombs at Sakkara [Nen-cheftka and Kagemeni, from the 5th Dynasty] and can also be seen on the western wall of the Luxor Temple.

The Ancient Egyptian ballet, in its lining-up and movements, used to be ordered like a chess play, since we always find nearby a repre-

sentation of a chess board.
Present-day Egyptian Dervishes are well known for their excellent whirl dancing, which has its particular mystical significance.

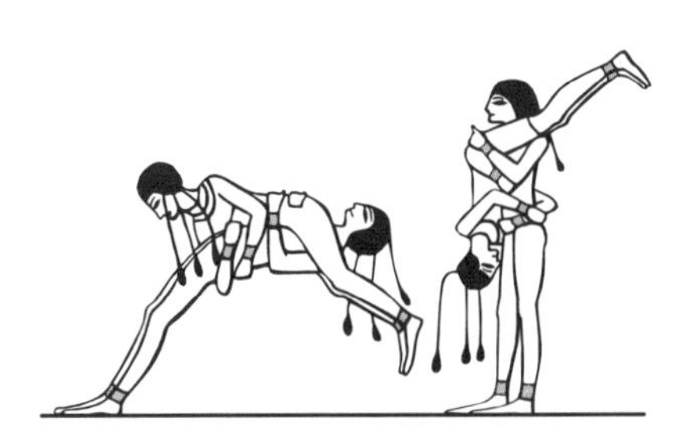

3. **Acrobatic.** The acrobatic dance was/is not a mere gymnastic exercise, but had/has important functions.

[Depicted scenes herein are from the tombs of Beni Hassan from the Middle Kingdom era.]

The leap dance presents one of the most popular motifs. In farming, the lead dancer identifies himself with what is planted. The higher the leap, the taller the corn will grow. Interestingly, this idea exists in the German sower tradition, as well as in the English, the Bohemian, and the Bulgarian.

4. Exhilaration Dancing.

The goal of the exhilaration dance is the attainment of a state of ecstasy in which the dancer transcends the human and physical and achieves ecstatic liberation from the self. This type of dancing is used in many occasions, such as treating a sick person, for initiation, or while sacrificing an animal [some applications are indicated in chapter 21]. The depicted scene above comes from **Ta-Apet** (Thebes) from the New Kingdom era.

The attainment of the state of ecstasy is reached through a well composed consecutive series—**Dor**. The selected sequence of modes causes the person(s) to levitate to higher realms by using music, singing, and dancing, in a well staged process.

Dancing Formations

Dancing formations can be done in lines, circles (round), solos, with partners, groups, etc. The group stands in line with a row of men opposite to a row of women. They could then form labyrinths, processions, solo dances, and couple dances, or a few would step into the circle for a few minutes of performance.

The round formation may have in the middle a person and/or an object (or sacrificial animal), whose power is supposed to radiate to those on the circle or vice versa.

Shown below are some dancing combinations
from the Old Kingdom era at Sakkara.

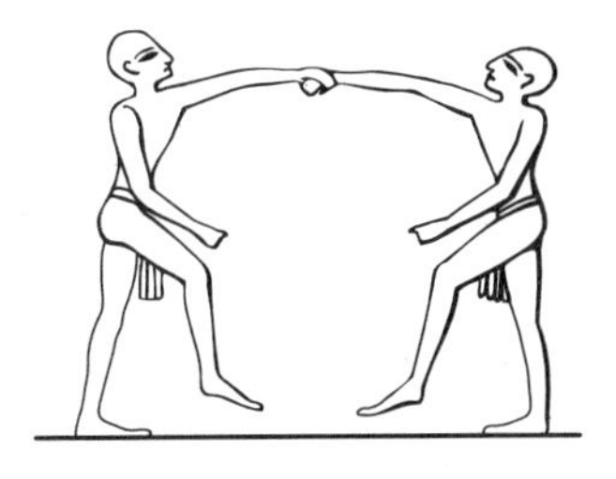

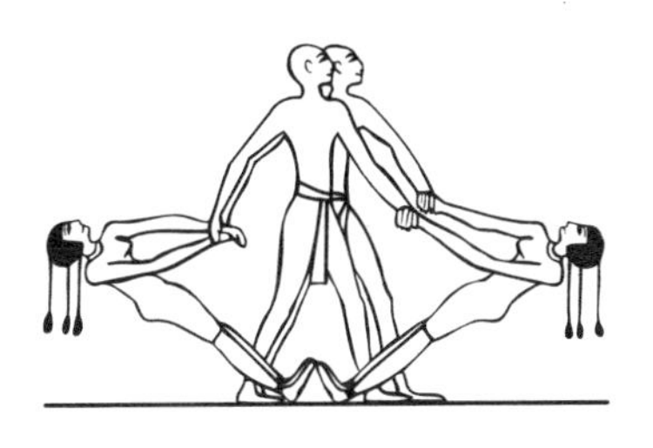

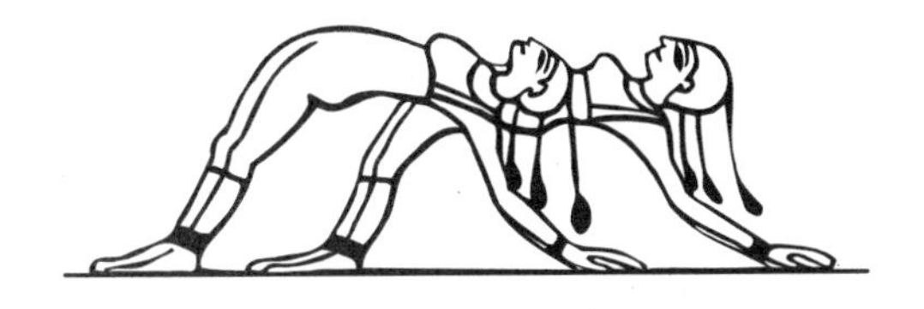

20

The Harmonic Practices

Musicians in Ancient (and Present-Day) Egypt

Musicians in Ancient and *Baladi* Egypt were/are highly regarded. The Ancient Egyptian **neteru** (gods) themselves are depicted on the temple walls, playing musical instruments. The profession of a musician was an obvious sign and practical consequence of the significant functions of music in the Egyptian society.

Musicians had various and distinctive roles. Some of their many musical titles included *overseer, instructor, director of musicians, teacher, musicians of* **Ma-at**–*mistress of the neteru, musicians of* **Amun**, *musicians of the Great Ennead, musicians of* **Het-Heru** *(Hathor)*, etc. The profession of the chironomid (conductor/maestro) was also noted in Ancient Egyptian literature.

The musical profession has comprised the whole range of representatives of the temples and other societal activities. There were various and well trained groups of singers and dancers who learned and practiced the set performance rules, suitable for the various occasions.

The Egyptians' model musician was **Heru** (Horus) **Behdety**, whose Greek rendering is *Apollo*. Diodorus of Sicily wrote about **Heru Behdety** and his nine muses—well trained in various arts associated with music, in *Book I* [18, 4-5]:

Heru Behdety listening to the harpist [now at the Louvre]

> *Ausar (Osiris) was laughter-loving and fond of music and the dance; consequently he took with him a multitude of musicians, among whom were **nine maidens** who could sing and were trained in the other arts, these maidens being those who are called **the Muses**; and their leader (hegetes), as the account goes, was Heru Behdety (Apollo), who was for that reason also given **the name Musegetes**.*

Diodorus' account provides us with two interesting points:

1. The title of **Heru** (Horus) **Behdety** is noted as **Muse-gete-s**, which is an Egyptian term, meaning *musician*. **Muse-gete/Muse-kate** is not an Arabic word.
2. The concept of nine muses is of Egyptian origin, as it relates to Ancient Egyptian deities.

Musicians in present-day Egypt belong to the mystical Sufi groups, specifically Dervishes. They perform in weddings, circumcisions, mouleds, funerals, etc. They are all well disciplined musicians, dancers, reciters, and singers, just like their ancestors. If they are not blind, they perform with blindfolded or closed eyes.

In the Ancient Egyptian musical scenes, most musicians are shown blind, vision impaired, or blindfolded—to exalt the metaphysical aspect of music.

The Temple Musical Activities

The Egyptian temple was the link, the proportional mean, between the macrocosmos (world) and microcosmos (man). It was a stage on which meetings were enacted between the **neter** (god) and the King, as a representative of the people. It was the place in which the cosmic energy, **neter** (god), came to dwell and radiate its potency to the land and people.

The temple's rituals were based upon and coordinated with the movements of the heavens, which were in turn manifestations of the divine cosmic law—**Ma-at**.

Sound related activities were the means to communicate with the supernatural forces of the universe. The vocal voice of the priests and the musical orchestras were sounding bridges between the macro- and the microcosmos—between the world of **neteru** (gods) and ancestors—and the world of the earthly living.

In Ancient Egypt, temples were commonly provided with recitation priests (chanting), and a complement of male and female musicians, singers, and dancers—all of whose task it was to participate in the various daily and seasonal cycles of rituals, so as to attune to the universal harmony.

At the religious ceremonies and processions, certain musicians attached to the priestly order were employed for the exclusive service of the temple.

Egyptian women participated in the performance of temple rites that included singing, instrument playing, and dancing. These female performers were generally daughters of the priests and nobles of the society—a reflection of the high regard for this profession.

The depicted scene [shown herein] from the 18th Dynasty [now at the Leiden Museum] shows temple musicians and a priest offering incense—as a part of the religious rituals.

In addition to the temple rituals, there were public festivities associated with temple activities, which were celebrated with singing, music and dancing. The festivities were of a diverse nature, and all followed very strict rules as per Plato, *Laws VII* [798e-799b] [see text on page 156].

Samples of some temple related festivities with musical significance were:

1. Oratory allegorical plays, which were directed by the temple priests, on open-air stages in front of the temples or on the temple ramps.

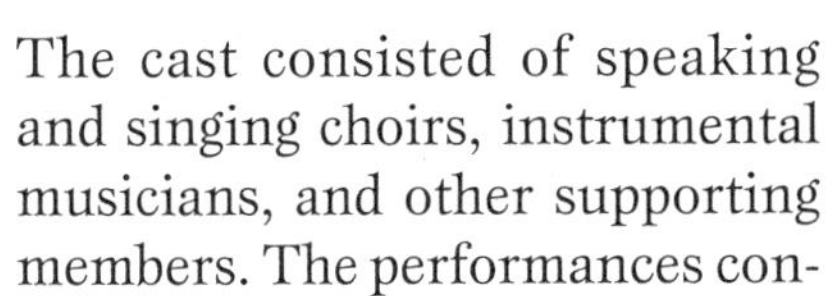

The cast consisted of speaking and singing choirs, instrumental musicians, and other supporting members. The performances consisted of various forms of recitations, choirs, or duets, in a musically shaped series of rhythmically narrated compositions—**Dor**.

The most famous story of **Auset** (Isis) and **Ausar** (Osiris) was played annually at the steps of the **Abtu** (Abydos) temple. It was the Model Story, full of all facets of knowledge. [Read about different aspects of this Model Story in *Egyptian Cosmology: The Animated Universe*, by same author.]

The same type mystery plays are still being performed in present-day Egypt during the *Mouleds*, by the mystical Egyptian Sufi groups. Mystery plays are now known as folkloric storytelling.

2. The **Apet** Festival celebrated the one mile (2 km) journey of **Amen's** ark—from his sanctuary at Karnak Temple to the temple of Luxor and back again. Scenes from an **Apet** Festival, celebrated during the time of Tut-Ankh-Amen, decorate the walls of a colonnade in the Luxor Temple, and give a lively impression of the occasion of musical and dancing performances.

The same celebration continues in present-day Egypt, by the *Baladi* Egyptians—performing the same ancient festivities, under a very thin layer of Islam.
The more things change, the more they stay the same!

3. Herodotus wrote about the **b.st** temple of Bubastis, right outside Zagazig, in the Nile Delta. The annual festivities of this ancient city attracted more than 700,000 people, singing, dancing, and having a great time. Herodotus described the happiness of the people, celebrating **Bast**, the symbol of Joy.

In the *Litany of* **Ra**, **Ra** is described as *The One of the Cat*, and as *The Great Cat*. The nine realms of the universe are manifested in the cat, for both the cat and the Grand Ennead (meaning nine-times-unity) have the same Ancient Egyptian term **b.st**. The nine realms are hosted by the nine muses.

The same festivities go on now, under a thin layer of Islam, as a *mouled* celebration.

4. The annual Musical Pilgrimage, as described next.

The Annual Musical Pilgrimage

Het-Heru (Hat-hor) means *House of* **Heru** *(Horus)*. In Egypt, when a man marries, he is *housed*—he becomes settled. The temple of **Het-Heru's** consort, **Heru** (Horus)—in his form as **Heru** (Horus) **Behdety**—is at Edfu. **Heru Behdety** was described as the **Musegate-s** (Musician), who was the leader of the nine muses.

Het-Heru (Hathor) was/is known as the *Mistress of Dance* and the *Mistress of Music*. **Het-Heru** (Hathor) is associated with the seven natural tones of the diatonic scale and is/was called *The Seven* **Het-Heru**. **Het-Heru's** (Hathor's) most important shrine is located at Dendera.

Each year, there was an immense reciprocal festival, with pilgrimages to and from the temples at Edfu and Dendera, and with joyous celebrations.

Both temples were built before the dynastic era (i.e. over 5,000 years ago). They, like other temples in Egypt, were restored/rebuilt every few centuries, to counter their aging process.

The annual musical pilgrimage began at Dendera, where the effigy of **Het-Heru** (Hathor) would embark each New Year, south towards Edfu. The effigy of **Heru** (*Horus*) would leave Edfu and head northward. Both would meet at the halfway point, between Dendera and Edfu. Jointly, they journeyed to the Edfu temple. After a short stay, the effigy of **Het-Heru** (Hathor) would return back to Dendera.

The symbolism of this annual musical pilgrimage relates to every couple, because **Heru** (Horus) and **Het-Heru** (Hathor) represent the husband and wife—in perfect harmony.

Public Activities

Several musical activities were mentioned throughout this book. The following are some additional samples of public related activities:

1. The ritual of the setting up of the **Tet** (Djed) pillar, which symbolizes the backbone of **Ausar** (Osiris), was the earliest "maypole" ritual.

   The presentations in the tomb of Kheriuf give us a variety of informative knowledge about many details relevant to this ceremony. Such scenes depict a whole program of music, dance, and singing performances.

2. **Farming Activities:** Musical and dancing rituals had/have an important role in the seasonal round of agricultural activities, such as the sowing of seeds, threshing, and harvesting.

   The Egyptian belief in Animism binds the action of man to surrounding nature. Man, who is rooted so inextricably in nature, and bound by destiny so close to earth, sea, trees, and animals, cannot place himself on the outside, in his activity or in his thought. Sowing and copulating, germinating and bearing, harvesting and delivering are interrelated and linked to human vitality and fertility.

   The Egyptian Pharaoh participated in agricultural activities and was called the *Lord of Corn/Our Crop/Our Harvest*, etc. Each year, the King hoed the first plot of farming land and sowed the first seeds. If the Pharaoh did not perform the daily liturgy to the **neteru** (gods/goddesses), the crops would perish.

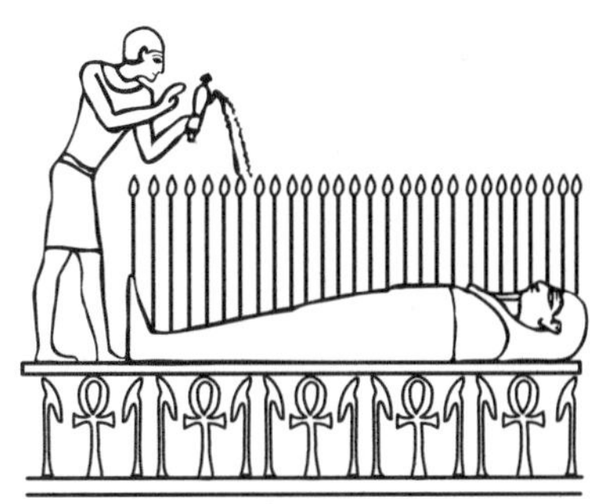
The Resurrection of the Wheat depicts **Ausar** with 28 stalks of wheat growing out of his coffin.

Based on his extensive training with the powers of the supernatural, the Pharaoh's body was believed to be charged with a divine dynamism that communicated itself to everything he touched. It was, therefore, his main function—to act as an intermediary between the natural and supernatural worlds, by conducting rites and sacrifices.

While the King and the priests had specific ritual duties related to agricultural activities, all farmers followed complementary rituals.

Several scenes that date back to the Old Kingdom mark the ritual singing for the first or the last sheaf. In several of these tombs, there are portrayals that show the corn harvest, accompanied by music. Examples are:

- In the tomb of Mereruka in Sakkara, there is a musician who blows the reed pipe, between the corn reaping farmers.
- In the tomb of Kahif (Giza, Old Kingdom), a singer is shown *singing* to the sheaf.
- Scenes of singing and playing the *nay* (flute) during the reaping are depicted in several other tombs.

Singing and dancing also accompanied the pressing of grapes, as depicted in several tombs in Sakkara, since the Old Kingdom era.

Scenes of harvest with the playing of sticks are found in several tombs in Sakkara, from the Old Kingdom era [ca. 2700 BCE]. They show long rows of boys or young men, who either stride out in big steps, or in a rhythmic dance step performing a sort of round dance or "procession". These presentations are often found near the harvest scenes, because of its close association with such activities. [More info on page 145.]

The tradition of stick-playing is widely spread in Egypt until now.

3. **Fishing:** Plato and others noted that the Egyptians not only caught, but tamed fish, with the same skill as they did land animals. Texts of fishermen's songs were found confirming Aelian's description of how the Thrissa fish of Lake Mareotis *"was caught by singing to it, and by the sound of crotala (clappers) made of shells. . ."* and how *"dancing up, it leapt into the nets spread for the purpose, giving great and abundant sport."*

Present-day Egyptian fishermen follow the same singing and dancing customs.

21

The Harmonic Sound Man

The Earthly Voyage

To stay in harmony with nature, the Ancient Egyptians utilized music and dance in all aspects of their personal earthly voyage—from the cradle to the grave, such as initiation ceremonies, medical/holistic treatments, etc. Here are a few examples:

1. **Infant naming** occurred/occurs seven days after birth (octave). Specific rituals, which include singing and dancing, were/are made for both boys and girls.

2. **Puberty rites.** The ceremony of male circumcision marks the immature boy's transformation, from a child to a man. Specific rituals and parade were/are usually performed during the *Mouleds*.

3. **Marriage ceremonies.** Special ceremonies were/are made to ensure the proper transfer from a single to married status, for both the man and woman. The two families also perform special rituals—to tie the knot in some ways—between each other.

4. **Restoring the Human Harmony**. Just like the vibrant universe, the human body as a whole is an immensely complex vibratory system. Everything is in a constant dynamic state of movement that is intimately connected to the rhythms, harmonies and pulsations of the universe. Each individual's internal biological clock not only follows solar, lunar, tidal, and seasonal cycles, but also follows cycles that are related to the basic periods of the planets as seen from earth. If a person's orderly rhythmic patterns were disturbed, this was an indication of trouble ahead. When out of tune, the body was seen as unhealthy or diseased.

   Het-Heru's (Hathor) temples were often healing centers, such as **Het-Heru's** main shrine at Dendera, where all manner of therapies were practiced, just like a hospital in our modern sense, more or less, but with more emphasis on healing the body and soul using all means, and not limited to surgical procedures.

   Het-Heru represents the intimate relationship between music, dancing, and the well-being of people.

   To heal a person is to restore the inner balance, by bringing that person back into tune. Music and dancing are sometimes needed, in conjunction with medical and surgical procedures.

   Music, singing, chanting, and dancing generate sonar fields, and soundwaves are now utilized more and more in surgical procedures. There are different types of soundwaves that can be used for different purposes. An example is the ultra-soundwaves, which cannot be detected by our ears, but doctors use its power as a kind of knifeless scalpel in microsurgery.

   The vocal powers generate soundwaves that can have

similar impacts on the vibratory system of the bodily organs. The vocal powers should not and cannot be underestimated. Witness the powerful voice of the soprano singer, who can shatter a glass with her voice.

Incantation and poetic chanting are scientifically controlled soundwaves that generate sonar fields, establishing an immediate vibratory identity with the essential principle that underlies any object or form. By pronouncing certain words or names of powers, in the proper manner and in the proper tone of voice, a priest/doctor could heal the sick.

If it is thought that an "evil spirit" has possessed a person, an exorcist with a greater degree of specialization may be called in. This treatment practice is known by the Egyptian term, *Zar*, which means a visit by a foreign spirit.

The treatment consists of, among other things, musical and dancing rituals. It is led by a specialist (usually a female), who is transported far from the physical, and connects the past and the future. She ascends to the spirits who threaten the well-being of man and struggles with them, until they give up and release their victim.

The sick person may be placed in the center of a circle of dancers, until the dancers in an ecstatic state have overpowered the spirit of sickness, chased it away, or even drawn it into themselves and conquered it.

In special cases, it may be the sick person himself who dances to get well. The sick person dances faster and faster within the circle of recitals of carefully composed sequences of melodies—**Dor** (to take him/her to higher and/or lower realms)—until the sickness spirits escape or are captured and sent away.

Death and Resurrection

Upon death, the person departs from earthly existence to another type of existence. Such a transition requires the proper sending off—commonly known as *funerary rites*.

The Egyptian Model Story of **Ausar** (Osiris) and **Auset** (Isis) provides the basis—among other things—for what to do after death. The Model Story portrays the two sisters, **Auset** (Isis) and **Nebt-Het** (Nephthys), as the guiding angels of all dead people—through the Duat, towards resurrection.

Auset and **Nebt-Het** performed ritualistic singing, to bring the deceased (**Ausar**) to [permanent] life—resurrection, i.e. to help the transition of the departed soul into the new metaphysical realm.

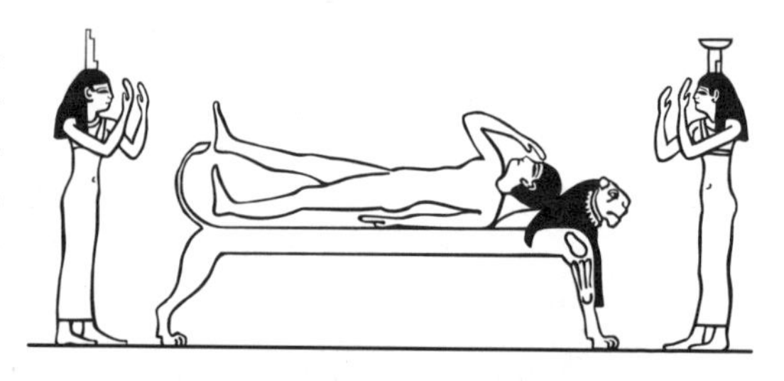

Auset (Isis) and **Nebt-Het** (Nepthys) in the resurrection rituals of **Ausar** (Osiris)

The two sisters serve as the model for present-day *Baladi* Egyptian *Enumerators*—specially trained women who sing specifically arranged series of funerary/transformational compositions (suite—**Dor**), which consists of distinct musical patterns and rhymes.

The first step in the funerary process is to reunite the deceased (at realm 8) with each's "Siamese" twin (at realm 9), who "apparently" separated at birth. The *Baladi* Egyptian Enumerators describe how the deceased is being prepared to join his/her counterpart (of the opposite sex), AS IF it is a marriage ceremony. [More about transformational (funerary) texts and process in *Egyptian Cosmology: The Animated Universe*, by same author.]

Music and dancing also played/play an important role, during and after the funeral procession. An example is depicted in the tomb of Ti [5th Dynasty], where the usual dance escort of the burial is shown.

Funeral dances make it possible for the soul of the deceased to find his/her ancestors.

Ritualistic music and dance are found in the Ancient Egyptian tombs of the "nobles". These people were/are *noble* in the sense of *noble characteristics*, not wealth. These special people have been and are called **Wali-s**, meaning *caretakers*. They are considered to be the intermediaries between the earthly living beings and the supernatural (heavenly realms), who come to earth to help others. As such, upon their departure from earthly living, they are sent off in festive celebrations, because the people recognize that they will soon have "a friend in a higher place" who can help them in their daily lives. Consequently, the **Wali-s**, then and now, are accompanied by music and ritual dances, in their funeral processions.

After the noble **Wali-s** leave earth, people continue to communicate with them at each's shrine. The communication is very special on his/her annual *mouled*, where the Sufis lead the activities with ritualistic recitation, singing, and dancing. The official annual number of *mouleds* in Egypt, even though it is contrary to Islam, is estimated at more than 3,000.

Ancient traditions endure. . . And The Beat Goes On

22

And The Beat Goes On

It has been written and repeated, that the Ancient Egyptians accepted the domination of the Ptolemaic and Roman rules (332 BCE - 642 BCE), that they had willingly changed their religious beliefs into Christianity, and a short time later, they willingly accepted Islam as a substitute for Christianity. Accordingly, many conflicting sides, who use Ancient Egypt to promote each's own agenda, insist that the ancient beliefs and traditions have died. The truth is that the ancient beliefs and traditions never died, and they continue to survive within the silent majority—the *Baladi* people of Egypt. Even though the loud minority—the *Afrangi* (meaning *foreign-like*) Egyptians—dominate the spotlight in government, academia, the media, etc, the *Baladi* Egyptians continue to maintain their ancestral traditions.

Because of the ironclad control of Islam over history writing since 642 CE, Moslem historians publicize that Egyptians forgot their identity and became a part of a big happy family called "Arabs". No one can dare oppose the line that Islam "saved" Egypt from the previous *Gahe-Liya* (ignorance era). As a result, we witness an intellectual state of terrorism that conceals realities into a cloud of dust.

The *Baladi* Egyptians, however, learned to survive playing with an egg and a stone (so to speak), so as to maintain the ancient traditions, under a thin layer of Islam. In other words, to give the "devil" its due—in lip service—in order to survive. [Maintaining their ancestral traditions, was noted in chapters 3 and 21, as well as countless examples referred to, in other chapters of the book.]

The Ancient Egyptian knowledge and practice of rhythm went underground when the Arabs invaded Egypt in 640 CE. Later, when the ironclad Islamic fist loosened a bit, musical texts appeared in Arabic language—since the Arab invaders outlawed the indigenous languages of their conquered countries such as Egypt.

In order to ignore the role of Ancient Egypt in the history of music, Western academia tells us that out of thin air the Arabized people possessed a musical system of rhythm and mensural values, as early as the 7th century CE. This system did not come out of thin air, but it was an actual existing system. The content and style of such musical treatises, written in the language of the invaders—Arabic—leads us to one source—Ancient Egypt.

All these early treatises (from the 7th to 12th century CE) about music included pure Egyptian terms and systems that were practiced in Ancient Egypt. These texts—written in Arabic—discussed existing practices that were passed on from previous generations (not out of thin air, and not out of Greece). All earlier Arabic writings had Egyptian terms. In later centuries, several musical terms gradually changed to Arabized words.

As the facts are laid out throughout this book since the Pharaonic Era, one will find that "Arabic" or "Islamic" music is baseless fiction. [See Appendix E for more info.] The "Arabized" writers of these documents never claimed that they invented anything. Yet Western academia awarded them titles, such as “theorists”, “inventors”, ...etc. They were nothing more than eyewitness reporters, recording what they heard.

The combined evidence of the Ancient Egyptian’s representations in temples and tombs, the numerous found Ancient Egyptian instruments, the early accounts of Greek and Roman writers, together with modern practices of *Baladi* Egyptians, proves that Egypt was the original source of all the so-called Arabic (and Persian) treatises. This combined evidence also proves that the ancestral chain of Egyptian traditions were never broken.

The Ancient Egyptian traditions endure, which confirms the accounts of ALL early historians, that the Egyptians are remarkably traditionalists to a fault. Early historians have witnessed this fact, such as:

Herodotus, in *The Histories, Book Two, 79*, states:

The Egyptians keep to their native customs and never adopt any from abroad.

Herodotus, in *The Histories, Book Two, 91*, states:

The Egyptians are unwilling to adopt Greek customs, or, to speak generally, those of any other country.

Egypt endures...And the Beat Goes On.

Appendices

Western Musical Tampering (Not "Tempering")

In chapter 9, both the cyclic and divisive methods of tuning musical instruments were discussed. It was also found that the Egyptian comma explains both the siamese twin nature of tones and the divergence in tuning results of musical string instruments.

Western musicologists considered the comma to be a mistake of creation that must be corrected. Curt Sachs, in his book, *Our Musical Heritage* [pgs 15-16], states:

> ***The irreconcilable divergence between the two methods (cyclic and divisive) harassed the music of the West*** *no less than that of the East, until the equal temperament, or division of the octave into twelve equal semitones, at last did away in the 18th century with the dubious so-called 'natural' intervals. Temperament, or tuning compromise, in some form, however, is neither a western nor a modern achievement. It exists everywhere and in every time, now as a spontaneous, now as* ***a willful alteration of nature****.*

This *"willful alteration of nature"* resulted from the notion that simple arithmetic must overrule the beauty of natural sounds.

The "simplification" of numbers is reflected now in the so-called "tempered" scale, whereby as per Alexander J. Ellis' [19th century] system, the whole octave of 1200 cents is divided into 12 equal semitones, each equal to 100 cents. Thus,

A semitone has	100 cents
A wholetone	200 cents
A minor third	300 cents
A major third	400 cents
A fourth	500 cents
A tritone (Augmented fourth)	600 cents
A fifth	700 cents
A minor sixth	800 cents
A major sixth	900 cents
A minor seventh	1000 cents
A major seventh	1100 cents
An octave	1200 cents

The statement of Curt Sachs on the previous page is incorrect, since:

1. Only those Western musicologists since the 19th century were/are "harassed" by the musical unit of the comma.

2. The term, *tempering*, should be replaced by *tinkering* or *fudging numbers*. This process did not change the fact that the Fifth (for example) is only perfect at 702 cents. Anything different than the natural sound value (say 700 cents for the Fifth) is not balanced.

After they committed this crime against music, Western musicologists began to demean—explicitly and implicitly—those other cultures, who continued/continue to follow the natural music, as being "primitive", of a "lower civilization", "Oriental", etc.

B

The Noise Makers

The Western Paradigms

John Anthony West, in his book, *The Travelers' Key to Ancient Egypt*, defined the causes of the common stereotyping of Ancient Egypt:

> *The study of Egypt has in general suffered from a quite unique form of double-barreled prejudice.*
>
> *[1] Religious scholars, whether Christian, Jewish, or Moslem, have been loathe to acknowledge Egypt as an important source of the most profound tenets of their respective creeds,*
>
> *[2] while rationalist scholars are equally loathe to acknowledge the existence of science and philosophy prior to the Greeks.*

Western academia suffers from both prejudices, because consciously or subconsciously, they refer to the biblical accounts as facts that require no scientific or scholarly scrutiny. There is no physical evidence to support the biblical accounts. Moreover, there was no dating of such accounts. As a matter of fact, only the Ancient Egyptians had an accurate calendar in the ancient world. This did not stop academia from making up dates for the unproven biblical events, in order to validate them as historical facts.

Here are excerpts from the books of the famed musicologist, Curt Sachs, affirming the Western paradigms:

> *The two pillars of European education during the Middle Ages and the Renaissance were theology and the classics.* ***Constantly dealing with the Holy Scriptures*** *and the books of Antiquity, the musical writers could not eschew at least a literary contact with the musical worlds of the Bible and of the Greeks. Much as they were engrossed in the musical problems of their days, in tuning, intervals, and counterpoint rules, they kept a loose connection with the half primitive half oriental sphere of either one. Even early treatises on music opened with a reverent if noncommittal bow to the Hebrews and Hellenes, to Miriam and David, to Pythagoras and the Roman Boethius.*
> ***So powerful was this education even in later times****.*
> *Sir John Hawkins, in his General history of the science and practice of music of the same year, went not even that far. In true cavalier fashion he did away with all the "barbarians." Their best music – as he wrote in the Preface – "is said to be hideous and astonishing sounds. Of what importance then can it be to enquire into a practice that has not its foundation in science or system."*
>
> *[Wellsprings - pg 5]*

> *The established historians of European music did not seek to expand their horizons beyond Europe, and their playground was the library with its manuscripts and printed scores.*
>
> *[Musicology - pg 42]*

> ***For the chapters on Greek and Hebrew music there were no witnesses and consequently no reports.*** *The two sections were easily filled with learned quotations from literary sources well known to all the author's erudite contemporaries; the music itself hardly needed discussion; being biblical or Greek, it was to every reader perfect almost by definition.*
>
> *[Musicology - pg 36]*

The latter half of the 20th century witnessed a change in style but no change in attitude. Their descriptions of non-Europeans being "barbarians", "lower civilizations", "primitive", ...etc. are now replaced with politically correct terms, but the attitudes did not improve—they actually became worse—implicit, condescending, and subtle.

Accreditation Without Justification

On the subject of Ancient Egypt, practically all Western academicians have contempt with envy towards this great civilization. The typical Western academician will simultaneously describe the achievements in Ancient Egypt as: 1) being borrowed/stolen/copied from non-Egyptians, and 2) describe Egyptians as being very conservative, who didn't change or evolve, who had no imagination, etc. This is irrational for a person to use contradictory arguments simultaneously.

The fact is that Egyptians (Ancient and *Baladi*) are traditionalist to a fault, as shown throughout the book, and as stated by Herodotus [see page 188].

As a consequence of their double prejudices, Western academia were/are eager to grasp at any straw, by giving credit for musical knowledge to anyone outside Egypt. Interestingly enough, these neighboring countries of Egypt never claimed to have this musical knowledge that Westerners give them credit for!!

A handful of performers that may appear foreign-looking are shown in a few Ancient Egyptian tombs. The presence of foreign-looking performers in Egypt—the most populous and richest country in the Old World—is not indicative of imported music and musicians. To assume (without evidence) the contrary, is a pathetic attempt to make the tail wag the dog. Western academia would never conclude that the presence of a non-European person playing in the Vienna Symphonic Orchestra means that Europe has imported its music and instruments from outside Europe! Furthermore, there is no evidence whatsoever that such instruments ever existed in any neighboring Asiatic country, at or prior to the time it was in use in Egypt. [An overview of Egypt's Asiatic neighbors are found in Appendices D and E.]

Western writing about the history of music in Egypt is infested with fact-twisting schemes. Examples are:

1. For the academician, the presence of a particular shape/form of an instrument in an Ancient Egyptian tomb that was not

found in an earlier Egyptian tomb, means that it was imported from an unspecified source! They fail to understand the simple fact that Ancient Egyptian tombs were not intended as a "documentary" of all shapes and forms of all Ancient Egyptian instruments.

2. Academicians use vague terms—in order to confuse—like, "Late Period", "Middle Ages", ...etc. They also shuffle the chronology of events, leaving out dates when convenient, etc. Hans Hickmann's references are masterpieces of intentional disorder and confusion.

3. When convenient, academicians recognize only written treatises that directly describe musical instruments and theory. Academicians call the people who wrote these documents *theorists*. Even though these writers never considered themselves as such. They were not and never claimed to be experts. They were conveying what the practicioners (musicians) told them.

Furthermore, academicians declared the birthplaces of such writers to be "cultural centers", when these places were nothing more than camel trading posts on trade routes, in the middle of the Asiatic wilderness.

4. Academia doesn't consider the absence of instruments, in their favorite Asiatic countries, to be an absence of evidence. They blame such absence on the climate of these Asiatic countries, which did not preserve the *fictional* instruments. This is a false premise, since the arid weather of Egypt is the same as that of its Asiatic neighbors.

5. In order to make unsubstantiated claims, academicians repeat what a previous academician wrote, even though the original writing is baseless or even fraudulent. [An example of such a scheme is shown on pages 202-3.]

6. The pan-Grecian conceit is another factor in the Western academic misrepresentation of facts about Ancient Egypt [see Appendix C].

The life of music, in Ancient Egypt, has transferred to other parts of the world, via:

1. International trade, such as with the Phoenicians, who were known as a seafaring, mercantile people. They were the transferring agents of material goods and culture, worldwide.

2. The numerous invaders of Egypt. No country was stolen from like Egypt was.

In order to verify the source of a musical instrument, one must provide the information and evidence to respond to the following queries:

1. When did instruments (or a particular musical system) appear in the different places? In other words, the evidence of instrument existence in one place before the other. Western academia made up dates for non-Egyptian sources, which did not even have an accountable calendar.

2. How and when was contact made between two different cultures (invasion, trade, etc)?

3. Do these types of instruments fit into this culture, such as their religious traditions, etc, or are they more or less "spoils of war"? Having "spoils of war" in the possession of the invaders of Ancient Egypt does not make them the inventors of musical theory and instruments.

4. Did the use of these instruments continue until now or did they disappear from existence, because they were never really a part of this culture?

When all these logical questions are answered honestly and completely, the Western accreditation of musical instruments to non-Egyptians will be shown as groundless.

Evidence is presented throughout the book, showing that Ancient Egypt had the knowledge, tools, and application prior to anyone else in the world. As such, we cannot waste paper refuting all the alleged accreditations of Western academicians.

C

The Pan-Grecian Conceit

Pythagoras Worshipping/Imprinting

Consistent with Western paradigms [noted in Appendix B], it was considered the "proper thing" to attribute all the sciences to the Greeks. This is contrary to the law of gradual and painful acquisition of scientific knowledge—that one period of a few centuries should have thus discovered everything.

In the process of making everything Greek, Western academicians use the terms, Greek this and Greek that, Pythagorean this or Pythagorean that, in every other sentence. By sheer forceful repetition of the terms, *Greek* and *Pythagorean*, they strive to make them facts.

It is a known fact that Pythagoras [ca. 580-500 BCE] studied for about 20 years in Egypt, soon after Egypt was open to Greek exploration and immigration, in the 7th century BCE.

Pythagoras and his immediate followers left nothing of their own writing. However, Western Academia attributed to Pythagoras and the so-called *Pythagoreans*, an open-ended list of major achievements. [More about Pythagoras and the Pythagorians in chapter 4.]

Yet the truth escapes from the very Western musicologists who wave the Pythagorean and Greek flags.

H.G. Farmer, in *Historical Facts* [pg 123], stated unequivocally what all his fellow European musicologists have discovered,

> *Pythagoras himself is said to have discovered or determined the numerical ratios of the fourth, fifth and octave, but the* ***account of the discovery*** *as given by Nikomachos, Gaudentios, Boethius, and others, is* ***so absurd that we are justified in considering the ascription to be spurious****.*

This is an oxymoron, by Western academicians, who advocate a greatness that they know does not exist. But there is more, as we will see next.

Western Academia and the Greek Writings on Music

Plato acknowledged and endorsed the Ancient Egyptian musical system. He established the Ideal Laws in his ideal *Republic*, based solely and exclusively on the Ancient Egyptian system—as referred to throughout the book.

Here are excerpts from Western academia that prove the useless state of the Greek writings about music:

- *The questions that Greek writers on music suggest, however, far outnumber those that they answer. The main trouble is the* ***impossibility of aligning the facts in chronological order:*** *admittedly or otherwise, the ancient authors* ***drew knowledge and opinions from different sources and mingled them carelessly with contemporaneous ideas. Contradictory, incomplete information written by non-specialists.***

  This fatal confusion of times, men, countries, and styles has mixed up terminology. Words like harmonia, eidos, tonos, tropos, systema were anything but clean-cut and are misleading rather than helpful. [Sachs – Rise - pg 201]

- *The Greeks started this confusion themselves; they misunderstood their own terms. The hopeless confusion of terms in*

*Greek theory, is reflected in **Plutarch's De anima, "the tones, tropes, or harmonies, or whatever you would call them**." [Sachs – Rise - p 216]*

- *The loss of the Principle has deprived them of an infinite knowledge. We are faced instead with ideas wrong or erroneous, of arbitrary calculations of these contradictory principles that swarm in their writings. [Roussier, Note XVI - §72]*

Western academia went even beyond distortion and deception to sheer fabrication of the physical evidence left by the Greeks. They wrote about Greek instruments that never existed. There is not a single **remain of Greek sculpture of an instrument furnished with a neck.** Father Montfaucon testified that in examining the representations of nearly 500 ancient Greek lyres, harps, and kitharas, he never met with one in which there was any contrivance for shortening strings, during the time of performance, as by a neck and fingerboard.

Western academia did not even hesitate to edit and re-edit the Greek treatises, in order to make the Greeks appear knowledgeable. Curt Sachs, in a moment of truth, uncovered some of the corrupted Western academic writings. In his book, *Rise of Music* [pages 232-233], Sachs describes an example of the dishonest academia, as follows,

> *The two series of harmoniai that could be performed with three different accordaturas of a pentatonic lyre at last exculpate Plutarch who, quoting a snappish criticism of the poet Pherekrates, relates that the boldest 'modern' composer of the fourth century BCE, Phrynis, gave the lyre a turning device in order to play no less than twelve harmoniai on five strings.*
>
> *Plutarch's 'editors' were utterly at sea with so cryptic an assertion. And they did what embarrassed philologists do: they emended the text. Burette averred that five strings, being an obvious understatement, "seven" must have been meant; Ulrici outdid his guess by printing "nine"; and Theodore Reinach, still unsatisfied, translated 'eleven'."*

The Egyptian Roots of Greek Knowledge

The Greeks themselves acknowledged Ancient Egypt as the source and the model for their Ideal Laws in their Ideal Republic. [Check references in the Index, under *Plato*, as well as throughout this book.] Some Western academicians acknowledge the foreign source of Greek music, as in the case of Curt Sachs' book, *The Rise of Music in the Ancient World* [page 216], when he summed it up as follows:

> ***The ancient Greek authors continually referred to older sources*** *the dates of which we do not know, and chronology is just as vague as terminology.*

1. The ancient Greek authors referred to older sources—namely the Egyptian **Dor-ians**. [Also see pages 40 through 43, and references to **Dor-ians** throughout the book.]

2. The Greeks did not date things because they had no accountable calendar.

The Greeks got another major opportunity to access Egyptian knowledge, when they came to Egypt [in the 7th century BCE] as mercenaries to fight off the Assyrians and Persians. [See Appendix D.] As a reward, they were allowed to settle in parts of Egypt. Herodotus wrote about these facts in *The Histories, Book Two* [154]:

> *To the Ionians and Carians who helped him to gain the throne Psammatichus granted two pieces of land, opposite one another on each side of the Nile...*
> *They were the first foreigners to live in Egypt, and after their original settlement there, the Greeks began regular intercourse with the Egyptians, so that we have accurate knowledge of Egyptian history from the time of Psammetichus onward. The docks and ruined houses of their first home, where they lived before Amasis moved them to Memphis, were still to be seen in my day.*

As stated earlier, practically all Greek notables went to Egypt for study, as reported by early Greek and Roman writers. [See Diodorus' account on page 41 of this book.]

The Arabic Greek "Connection"

As stated on pages 199-200, the Greek treatises were conflicting and obscured. Western academia decided to use the Arabized world as a "piggyback", in order to clarify the confused and obscured Greek treatises. The leader of this plot was H.G. Farmer, whose knowledge of the Arabic language was little and therefore dangerous. In order to impress his (non-Arabic) readers, he showed some Arabic text, claimed to be from Arabic treatises. However, any Arabic-speaking person, like the author of this book, can easily see the outright deceit of H.G. Farmer, whose displayed Arabic texts are written in 20th century style, not that of the time of these Arabic treatises and moreover, they are in typed form—not handwritten!! Notwithstanding the above, Farmer's assertions are contrary to the displayed text.

Farmer was busy threading an imaginary Arabic–Greek connection, and ignoring the Greek–Ancient Egyptian connection (such as the **Dor-ians**), as well as the adoption of the Ancient Egyptian musical system in Plato's Ideal Laws.

Farmer claimed that during the 8th and 9th centuries, the musical treatises of Aristoxenos, Aristotle, Euklid, Ptolemy and Nikomachos had been translated into Arabic and that Arabic treatises of the 9th century CE forward, were based on such Greek treatises.

Yet Farmer contradicts himself in his book, *The Sources of Arabian Music* [Leiden, 1965, page xx], where he stated,

> *To appreciate how there could have been a literary influence in the Arabian cultural contact, one must realize that there was not a solitary Greek work on the theory of music known during the period from the Anonymous II (4th century) until Psellos (11th century). It was only such Arabic authors as Al-Kindi, Al-Farabi, Ibn Sina, Ibn Zaila, Al-Sarakhsi, Ibn al-Haitham and others who were producing books on the theory of music from the 9th to the 11th century.*

In addition to the above contrary evidence, the following are additional points:

1. No evidence was provided to support Farmer's academic posturing and assertiveness.

2. Arabs considered anything outside Islam to be heretic. Consequently, they burned libraries and books. In other words, there was nothing left to translate.

3. None of these treatises that Farmer referred to, or displayed portions of, refer to Greece or any Greek person or writing.

4. Arabs hate foreign languages and whenever possible, they outlawed native languages of their conquered lands—as they did in Ancient Egypt. Arabs felt threatened by foreign languages.

Contrary to the repeated claims by non-Arabic-speaking Western academicians, the early Arab writers never claimed themselves to be "enthusiastic followers of the Greek role models".

Both the Greeks and Arabs had access to the supreme knowledge of the Ancient Egyptian music.

The continuous repetition of Farmer's unsubstantiated assertions by other academicians will never make fact out of fiction.

D

Pre-Islam Asiatic Neighbors

The Mirages of Sumer, Mesopotamia, Babylonia

Western musicologists begin the musical history at Sumer. References are made to no more than a handful of primitive engravings (whose authenticity is highly questioned), displayed in a Philadelphia university museum. Even if we accept their credibility, such engravings tells us nothing of value about music.

With no accountable calendar in Sumer, or any of its neighboring Asiatic lands, Western musicologists fabricated dates for these insignificant items, to make them as old as the known history of the Egyptian dynastic era. In doing so, academia can thus equate Sumer—in spite of its lack of evidence—to the richness of the Ancient Egyptian civilization.

Then, they used the biblical Abraham, saying he may have come from Sumer, as a prime example of a connection between Sumer and Ancient Egypt, so as to imply that the Egyptian civilization is indebted to Sumer. Yet the Bible tells us that Abraham came to Egypt to escape the famine in the "highly civilized" Sumer!

Similar fictional tales are told by Western academia, about the "highly civilized" Mesopotamia and Babylon regions.

The Assyrians

The Assyrians were known as fierce and ruthless warriors with a voracious appetite for war and destruction. The Assyrians invaded Egypt several times in the 7th century BCE and pillaged it. Years later, Greek and Carian mercenaries were hired by the Egyptians to defeat and push the Assyrians out of Egypt.

The only known archeological findings of these warmongers is situated in the immediate vicinity of Mosul, on the opposite bank of the Tigris. A collection from Nineveh is now exhibited in the British Museum, together with a handful of slabs from Kouyunjik. Such collections are dated to about 600 years BCE, i.e. shortly after their return from Egypt.

The wall reliefs (which are not a part of any religious temples) were basically no more than a recording of their spoils of war.

The reliefs [example shown herein] show some musical instruments that were in use in Egypt several centuries (millennia) before 600 BCE.

Several pieces of sculptured ivory are clearly of Egyptian origin, such as:

- A figure of the Egyptian **netert Het-Heru** (goddess Hathor), holding a lotus-flower in her left hand, and with the typical Ancient Egyptian winged sun over her head.
- Several flat cups or dishes of copper, which are ornamented with Egyptian figures. One bears the winged sphinx wearing the double crown of Egypt, and the winged sun, together with the scarab with outstretched wings, and the sun disk between its front feet.

The Persians

The Persians invaded Egypt several times:

- The Persians under Cambyses invaded and occupied Egypt in 525 BCE. Cambyses ruled for 3 years. Cambyses, and his subsequent Persian rulers, admired Egypt and tried to blend in with the Ancient Egyptian society, but were rejected by the Egyptians and expelled in 404 BCE.

- The Persians came back to Egypt in 343 BCE. The Egyptians sought outside help and in 323 BCE, Alexander and his Macedonian soldiers expelled the Persians again out of Egypt.

- The Persians came back during the Byzantines rule in 616 CE and withdrew out of Egypt in 628 CE.

The earliest musical evidence in Persia is an illustration of a harp, depicted on old sculptures that exist on a rock, called Tackt-i-Bostan, situated in the vicinity of the town of Kermanshah, and dated towards the end of the 6th century CE (i.e. much later than Ancient Egypt). It is therefore clear that a wall relief of a harp was not a part of their musical system, but was a spoil of war after their numerous invasions of Egypt from 600 BCE to 650 CE.

After reviewing the questions on page 197, and the dating of the Ancient Egyptian instruments presented in Part 4 of this book, one will conclude that all Persian musical instruments and practices were present in Ancient Egypt long before Persia or any other culture.

The Persians, since Cambyses, have shown their great admiration for Ancient Egypt. It is no wonder then, that the names of several Egyptian instruments were maintained by Persians. The similarity in name of some instruments (such as *nay*, rababa, etc) and musical terms is due to the Persians' adoption of the Ancient Egyptian knowledge.

[More about the post-Islam era of Persia in Appendix E.]

The Hebrews

In parts of the Old Testament, references are made to musical instruments and practices that occurred only during a particular era—which as we will see, is totally related to Ancient Egypt.

The Pentateuch (the first five books of the Old Testament) makes little mention of music. Then there was a sudden influx of musical life, during the alleged times of the biblical David and Solomon. But just as sudden, everything disappeared two generations later. This sudden "change" can only be due to foreign influence—Ancient Egypt.

Here are certain facts about the period of sudden musical life in the Bible:

1. The instruments (mentioned in the Bible during this era) have never been pictured.

2. No archeological discovery to date allows a supposition of the existence of such instruments.

3. The identities and shapes of the instruments stated in the Bible were already forgotten at the time of the Second Temple.

4. Ancient Egypt, during this era, was the sole source of musical richness. The Bible itself admits to the presence of a very rich musical life in Egypt. Examples are:

   a. The biblical character, Moses himself, who had been brought up by the Pharaoh's daughter, *"was learned in all the wisdom of the Egyptians"* [Acts vii. 22]; and the singing of the children of Israel before the golden calf after their departure from Egypt [Exodus xxxii. 18] was in the Egyptian manner.

   b. The Talmud admits that the Egyptian princess, whom the biblical character, Solomon, took for wife, brought a thousand musical instruments in her dowry—indicative of the richness of the Egyptian musical life.

c. Despite the hard work of biblical scholars, historians and archeologists, no single piece of evidence has been found to support the biblical accounts of the period of the alleged United Monarchy of David and Solomon.

The historical evidence from Ancient Egypt shows that both the biblical David and Solomon (as well as Moses) were Egyptian Pharaohs from the 18th Dynasty. [See *Historical Deception: The Untold Story of Ancient Egypt*, by same author, for details.]

E

The Post-Islam Arabized/ Islamized World

Islamic Music: An *Oxymoron*

After the death of Mohammed (632 CE), his followers conquered many lands. They forced their new-found religion—Islam and their own language—Arabic, on their conquered peoples.

Western academia tells us that in the post-Islamic era, a peculiar type of music that is associated with a religion (such as Islam), or language (such as Arabic), came into existence. Such notions are incorrect, because:

1. There is no *"Music of Islam"*, as much as there is almost no music of Catholic, Protestant or Greek-Orthodox as such. Islam, as a religious community, comprises many peoples, states and language areas.

Peoples converted into Islam do not necessarily have a corresponding music. This is clearly evident in the Islamicized minorities of China or Africa, whose music has no resemblance whatsoever to other parts of the Islamized countries.

2. Music in Islam is considered one of the "forbidden pleasures". Even listening to music is a sinful act. All treatises on Islamic laws forbid music.

3. There has never been a real (religious) music of Islam. Even the call for prayers from mosques is barely tolerated by the orthodox Moslem. Even the recitation of the Koran in the individual countries is carried out differently in each area.

Out of Egypt

The history of music in the Arabized/Islamized world is closely linked to the whim of the ruler and how he interprets/enforces Islamic laws. During certain periods, music was/is tolerated; during others, it was outlawed and condemned.

During "permissible" periods, some musical treatises appeared in Arabic—the only lawful language. (As stated earlier, the invading Moslem Arabs outlawed both the religion and language of their conquered countries—as in Egypt.) All these early treatises (from the 7th to 12th century CE), written in Arabic, about music, included pure Egyptian terms and systems that were practiced in Ancient Egypt. In later centuries, several musical terms changed to Arabic. [Examples are shown on pages 83 and 87 of this book.]

Since Islamic laws were stricter under Arab rulers, the un-Arabized countries like Persia had a freer hand. It was then safer for the people under the ironclad Arab rule, to point to non-Arabs as the source of the *Islamic outlawed* music. This is the reason one or two Arabized treatises wrote that the Persians possessed the knowledge of musical theory and practices. Furthermore, the evidence speaks against such remarks. Reviewing the dates and manner of appearance of instruments and musical practices leads us to one source only—Egypt.

Tight-stepped musical scales were attributed to post-Islam Persia and some Arabized areas. The evidence in Ancient Egypt shows that Egypt was the source of such scales. Based on evidence from the Old and Middle Kingdoms (5,000 years ago), the Ancient Egyptian instruments and the exhibited playing techniques [shown in Part 4 of this book] reveal several types of tight-stepped scales. In other words, such scales were not imported by the "Arabs" or Persians into post-Pharaonic Egypt, but logically the other way around—out of Egypt.

Glossary

antiphony – two different and alternating sounds, such as a response sung between a single voice and group of singers, or between two groups of singers, etc. [See more on page 158.]

Baladi – see page 13, item #6.

BCE – **B**efore **C**ommon **E**ra. Also noted in other references as BC.

beat – a constant pulsation. It acts as a ruler by which we can measure time.

buk-nunu – an Ancient Egyptian musical unit, equal to 7.55 cents. See **buk-nun** in Index for more information and details.

CE – **C**ommon **E**ra. Also noted in other references as AD.

cent – a standard unit for measuring musical intervals. An octave is equal to 1200 cents.

chironomid – one who gestures with his/her hands—a maestro/ conductor.

chironomy – the art of conducting or representing music by gestures of the fingers, hand(s), and/or arm(s).

chord – a combination of three or more tones sounded together in harmony.

comma – an Ancient Egyptian musical unit, equal to 22.64 cents. See comma in Index for more information and details.

diatonic – a scale consisting of 5 whole tones and 2 semitones.

dor – as a musical term, it means a musical composition organized in a series form; comparable to a musical suite. [See more on page 159.]

enharmonic – designating a ¼ step/note or less.

ethos – the expression of a mode that is connected to its structure. Describes the ethical power or moral force of a mode; its ability to influence the development of character and attitudes in the listener.

Fifth – can mean either: 1) the fifth tone of an ascending diatonic scale, or a tone four degrees above or below any given tone in such a scale—dominant. 2) the interval between two such tones, or a combination of them.

Fourth – can mean either: 1) the fourth tone of an ascending diatonic scale, or a tone three degrees above or below any given tone in such a scale—subdominant. 2) the interval between two such tones, or a combination of them.

fret – narrow, lateral ridges fixed across the finger board of a stringed instrument, such as a guitar, etc., to guide the fingering.

halftone – *see* semitone.

heptatonic – consists of seven (hepta) tones.

interval – can mean either: 1) the ratio of the number of vibrations between two different tones. 2) The distance separating two consecutive musical notes. [Also see *tone* and *semitone*.]

meter – succession of equal beats, characterized by the periodic return of a strong beat.

mode – a rhythmical system, consisting of its own unique combination of tones and rhythms, in order to provide specific influence on the listener. [Also see *ethos*.]

mouled/moulid – the annual "birthday" celebration of a **Wali** (folk saint) in Ancient and *Baladi* Egypt. [Also see ***Wali***.]

neter/netert – a divine principle/function/attribute of the One Great God. (Incorrectly translated as *god/goddess*).

notes – in Western musical terms, the letters *A* (*La*) to *G* (*Sol*) are used to designate notes.

onomatopoeic – the naming of a thing or action by a vocal imitation of sound associated with it (ex: *hiss*).

pentatonic – a scale consisting of five tones—three of which are wholetones, and two semitones—like that of the black keys on a keyboard.

perfect – the name given to certain intervals—the Fourth, Fifth, and Octave. The term is applied to these intervals in their natural sounds (not "tempered").

pitch – the position of a tone in a musical scale, determined by the frequency of vibration, and measured by cycles per second.

polyphony – the simultaneous sounding of different notes; the sounding of two or more different melodies simultaneously.

scale – any series of eight tones to the octave—arranged in a step-by-step rising or falling of pitch, which consists of a given pattern of intervals (the differences of pitch between notes).

semitone – the intervals between *B* (*Si*) and *C* (*Do*), and between *E* (*Mi*) and *F* (*Fa*). [Also see *tone*].

stanza – a group of lines of verse forming one of the divisions of a poem or song. It typically has a regular pattern in the number of lines and the arrangement of meter and rhyme.

step – interval of sound.

temperament – the rounding off of the values of the musical intervals, away from those of their natural values, to the nearest 100 cent number. Keyboard instruments are tuned to a scale of equal "temperament".

Tet – a symbolic pillar, representing the backbone of Ausar (Osiris)—the support of creation. It represents the channel through which the divine spirit might rise through matter to rejoin its source.

tetrachord – a series of four tones comprising a total interval of a Perfect Fourth; half an octave.

timbre – the quality or color of the sound invoked. It distinguishes one voice or instrument from another.

tone – the combination of pitch, intensity (loudness) and quality (timbre). The interval between each of the notes is a tone, except between *B* (*Si*) and *C* (*Do*), and between *E* (*Mi*) and *F* (*Fa*), where the interval is a semitone in each case.

tonality – the relationship between musical sounds or tones, taking into account their vibratory relationships and their appreciation by the ear. A systematic musical structure.

unison – the same sound, produced by two or more instruments or voices.

Wali – A saint-type person who the *Baladi* and Ancient Egyptians respect, visit, and ask favors. This concept is contrary to Islam. Wali-s are chosen by ordinary people, based on performance. Once the people can see that this person does indeed have the ability to influence supernatural forces, in order to assist those on earth, and as a result fulfills their wishes, then he or she is considered to be a Wali. [Also see *mouled/moulid*.]

Selected Bibliography

Blackman, Winifred S. *The Fellahin of Upper Egypt*. London, 1968.

Burney, Charles. *A General History of Music*, 2 volumes. New York, 1935.

Dio Cassius. *Roman History*, Vol 3. Tr. By E. Gary. London, 1914.

Engel, Carl. *The Music of The Most Ancient Nations*. London, 1929.

Erlanger, Baron Rodolphe. *La Musique Arabe*. Paris, 1930.

Erman, Adolf. *Life in Ancient Egypt*. New York, 1971.

Farmer, H.G. *The Sources of Arabian Music*. Leiden, 1965.

Farmer, H.G. *Historical Facts for the Arabian Music Influence*. New York, 1971.

Fétis, François Joseph. *Biographie Universelle des Musiciens et Bibliographie Générale de la Musique*. (Universal biography of Musicians). Bruxelles, 1837.

Gadalla, Moustafa. *Egyptian Cosmology: The Animated Universe*. USA, 2001.

Gadalla, Moustafa. *Egyptian Harmony: The Visual Music*. USA, 2000.

Gadalla, Moustafa. *Historical Deception: The Untold Story of Ancient Egypt - Second Edition*. USA, 1999.

Godwin, Joscelyn. *Harmonies of Heaven and Earth*. Rochester,

Vermont, USA. 1987.

Gretz, Ronald J. *Music Language and Fundamentals.* USA, 1994.

Haïk-Vantoura, Suzanne. *The Music of the Bible Revealed.* Tr. by Dennis Weber/Ed. by John Wheeler. Berkeley, CA, 1991.

Herodotus. *The Histories.* Tr. By Aubrey DeSelincourt. London, 1996.

Hickmann, Hans. *Musikgeschichte in Bildern: Ägypten.* Leipzig, Germany, 1961.

Hickmann, Hans. *Orientalische Musik.* Leiden, 1970.

Kepler, Johannes. *The Harmony of the World.* Tr. by E. J. Aiton. USA, 1997.

Lane, E.W. *The Manners and Customs of the Modern Egyptians.* London, 1836.

Levin, Flora R. *The Manual of Harmonics of Nicomachus.* Tr. and commentary by Levin, Flora R. Grand Rapids, Michigan, USA, 1994.

Levy, Ernst and Siegmund LeVarie. *Music Morphology – A discourse and dictionary.* Kent, Ohio, USA, 1983.

Levy, Ernst. *A Theory of Harmony.* Albany, New York, USA, 1985.

Levy, Ernst and Siegmund LeVarie. *Tone: A Study in Musical Acoustics.* Kent, Ohio, USA, 1980.

Lilienfeld, Robert. *An Introduction to Music.* New York, 1962.

Manniche, Lise. *Music and Musicians in Ancient Egypt.* London, 1991.

Plato. *The Collected Dialogues of Plato including the Letters.* Edited by E. Hamilton & H. Cairns. New York, USA, 1961.

Plutarch. *Plutarch's Moralia, Volume V*. Tr. by Frank Cole Babbitt. London, 1927.

Polin, Claire C. J. *Music of the Ancient Near East*. New York, 1954.

Roussier, Pierre Joseph. *Mémoire Sur La Musique Des Anciens*. Paris, 1770.

Sachs, Curt. *The History of Musical Instruments*. New York, 1940.

Sachs, Curt. *Our Musical Heritage*. Englwood Cliffs, NJ, USA, 1955.

Sachs, Curt, and others. T*he Place of Musicology in American Institutions of Higher Learning*. New York, 1977.

Sachs, Curt. *Rhythm and Tempo: A Study in Music History*. New York, 1953.

Sachs, Curt. *The Rise of Music in the Ancient World*. New York, 1943.

Sachs, Curt. *The Wellsprings of Music*. The Hague, Holland, 1962.

Sachs, Curt. *World History of Dance*. Tr. By Bessie Schönberg. New York, 1937.

Siculus, Diodorus. *Vol 1*. Tr. by C.H. Oldfather. London, 1964.

Signell, Karl L. *Makam Modal Practice in Turkish Art Music*. New York, 1986.

Stanford, C.V. and Forsyth, Cecil. *A History of Music*. New York, 1925.

Touma, H.H. *The Music of the Arabs*. Portland, Oregon, USA, 1996.

Wilkinson, J. Gardner. *The Ancient Egyptians: Their Life and Customs*. London, 1988.

Numerous references in Arabic language.

Sources and Notes

My references to the sources are listed in the previous section, Selected Bibliography. They are only referred to for the facts, events, and dates, not for their interpretations of such information. [Read Appendices for commentary on biases and distortions by Western academicians.]

1. Cosmic Consciousness

Kepler (*Harmony of the World*), Godwin
Gadalla (*Egyptian Cosmology, Historical Deception*)

2. Music All The Time (24 hours, 7 days)

Dio Cassius, Roussier

3. Diatonic Week

Dio Cassius, Godwin, Roussier, Blackman, Gadalla being a native Egyptian

4. Roots of Laws

Ideal Laws & Plato: Sachs (*Our Musical Heritage*), Plato, Diodorus
Roots of Greek Music: Practically all references recognize the two musical eras in Greek history
The Egyptian Dor-ians: Herodotus, Engel, Levin

5. Ma-at

Gadalla (*Egyptian Harmony*)

6. Tehuti, Divine Sound

Gadalla (*Egyptian Cosmology, Egyptian Harmony*), Plato, Roussier
Greek terminologies: Levin

7. Musical Model

Diodorus, Gadalla (*Historical Deception*, re. calendar)

8. Musical Dynamo

Gadalla (*Egyptian Harmony*), Plutarch, Diodorus, Roussier, Touma

9. The Musical Measuring Unit

Sachs (*Our Musical Heritage*), Gadalla (*Egyptian Harmony*), Gadalla being a native Egyptian

10. The Musical Frameworks

Sachs (*Our Musical Heritage, Rise of Music*), Roussier

11. Musical Structure

Moods and Modes: Moore, Plato
Design Characteristics: Sachs (*Our Musical Heritage*), Lilienfeld
Written Sounds: Plato, Engel, Fétis, Stanford/Forsyth, Burney

12. Musical Performance

Harmonic Hand: Gadalla (*Historical Deception, Egyptian Harmony*), Vantoura, Sachs (*Rise of Music*), Hickmann (*Orientalische Musik*), Hickmann (*Musikgeschichte in Bildern: Ägypten*)

Rhythmic Timing: Plato, Moore, Burney, Levy & LeVarie, Sachs (*Rise of Music*), Gadalla (*Egyptian Harmony*), Polin

13. The Wealth of Instruments

Pitches and Scales: Sachs (*History of Musical Instruments, Rise of Music*), Hickmann (*Musikgeschichte in Bildern: Ägypten, Orientalische Musik*)

Musical Orchestra: Wilkinson, Hickmann (*Musikgeschichte in Bildern: Ägypten, Orientalische Musik*)

Other Items: Gadalla (*Egyptian Cosmology, Egyptian Harmony*) and practically all references

14. Strings

Lyres: Polin, Engel, Wilkinson, Hickmann (*Musikgeschichte in Bildern: Ägypten*)
Lyres–Compass: Sachs (*History of Musical Instruments*), Hickmann (*Orientalische Musik, Musikgeschichte in Bildern: Ägypten*)
Tri-gonon/Ka-Nun: Hickmann (*Orientalische Musik*), Sachs (*History of Musical Instruments*), Egyptian literature in Arabic

Harps: Wilkinson, Polin, Hickmann (*Musikgeschichte in Bildern: Ägypten*) [specific examples in tombs]

Harp playing techniques: Hickmann (*Musikgeschichte in Bildern: Ägypten*), Sachs (*Rise of Music*)

Capacity of Harps: Manniche, Engel, Sachs (*History of Musical Instruments*), Burney

Neck Instruments: Engel, Sachs (*History of Musical Instruments*), Farmer [Arabized Era], Erlanger [Arabized Era], Hickmann (*Orientalische Musik, Musik-geschichte in Bildern: Ägypten*), Manniche, Polin, Wilkinson

Tuning pegs: Engel, Polin

2-strings: Burney (*Compass*), Hickmann (*Musikgeschichte in Bildern: Ägypten*) [samples in tombs]

3-strings: Engel, Manniche

4-strings: Engel

short-neck: Hickmann (*Musikgeschichte in Bildern: Ägypten*), Manniche

Egyptian Guitars: Hickmann (*Musikgeschichte in Bildern: Ägypten*), Engel, Wilkinson

Various examples in Ancient Egyptian tombs: Hickmann (*Musikgeschichte in Bildern: Ägypten*), Engel, Manniche

Bowed instruments: Hickmann (*Musikgeschichte in Bildern: Ägypten*), Touma, Wilkinson

15. Wind

Nay: Polin, Hickmann (*Musikgeschichte in Bildern: Ägypten*), Egyptian literature in Arabic, Sachs (*History of Musical Instruments*), Wilkinson, Engel

playing techniques: Engel, Sachs (*Wellspring*), Sachs (*History of Musical Instruments*), Hickmann (*Orientalische Musik*)

Examples in tombs: Hickmann (*Musikgeschichte in Bildern: Ägypten*)

Transverse Flute: Hickmann (*Musikgeschichte in Bildern: Ägypten*), Polin, Wilkinson, Sachs (*History of Musical Instruments*)

Pan Flute: Sachs (*History of Musical Instruments*), Hickmann (*Musikgeschichte in Bildern: Ägypten*)

Single Pipe: Wilkinson

Partial analysis of pipes in different museums: Sachs (*Rise of Music*)

Double Pipes: Stanford/Forsyth, Wilkinson, Hickmann (*Musikgeschichte in Bildern: Ägypten*), Manniche, Sachs (*History of Musical Instruments*), Wilkinson, Polin, Sachs (*Rise of Music*), Hickmann (*Orientalische Musik*)

The Two Horns: Polin, Hickmann (*Musikgeschichte in Bildern: Ägypten*), Sachs (*Wellsprings*)

Examples of horns: Hickmann (*Musikgeschichte in Bildern: Ägypten*)

16. Percussion Instruments

Membrano

Drums: Wilkinson, Hickmann (*Musikgeschichte in Bildern: Ägypten*), Engel, Polin

Abusir Drum: Sachs (*History of Musical Instruments*)

Tambourine: Wilkinson, Hickmann (*Musikgeschichte in Bildern: Ägypten*), Touma

Non-Membrano

Sticks: Hickmann (*Musikgeschichte in Bildern: Ägypten*), Sachs (*History of Musical Instruments*)

Clappers: Wilkinson, Hickmann (*Musikgeschichte in Bildern: Ägypten*), Polin

Sistrums (Sistra): Wilkinson, Hickmann (*Musikgeschichte in Bildern: Ägypten*)

Cymbals and Castanets: Polin, Hickmann (*Musikgeschichte in Bildern: Ägypten*), Wilkinson, Sachs (*History of Musical Instruments*), Stanford/Forsyth

Bells (Chimes): Sachs (*History of Musical Instruments*), Polin, Engel

Bells in museums and tombs: Hickmann (*Musikgeschichte in Bildern: Ägypten*)

Xylophone: Engel, Wilkinson

Human Parts: Wilkinson, Hickmann (*Musikgeschichte in Bildern: Ägypten*), Touma

17. The Universal Harmony

The Universal Music Balance: Lilienfeld, Plato

Antiphonies: Hickmann (*Orientalische Musik*, *Musikgeschichte in Bildern: Ägypten*), Manniche, and Sachs (*Rise of Music*)

The Dor-ian Suites: Touma, Egyptian literature in Arabic

18. The Vocal Powers

Generating Sounds: Burney, Levy & LeVarie, Blackman

Resonating through Head and Chest: Hickmann (*Orientalische Musik*, *Musikgeschichte in Bildern: Ägypten*), Sachs (*Rise of Music*)

Vocal Music Themes

Wilkinson, Touma, Hickmann (*Orientalische Musik*, *Musikgeschichte in Bildern: Ägypten*), Blackman, and Gadalla being a native Egyptian

19. Rhythmic Dancing

Lord of Dance: Gadalla (*Historical Deception*), Engel, Hickmann (*Musikgeschichte in Bildern: Ägypten*), Blackman

Dancing Types: Polin, Wilkinson, Sachs (*World History of Dance*)

Dancing Formations: Wilkinson, Engel, Hickmann (*Musikgeschichte in Bildern: Ägypten*), Sachs (*World History of Dance*), Egyptian literature in Arabic

20. The Harmonic Practices

Musicians in Ancient Egypt: Hickmann (*Musikgeschichte in Bildern: Ägypten, Orientalische Musik*), Wilkinson, Gadalla (*Historical Deception, Egyptian Cosmology*), Burney, Diodorus, Blackman

Temple Activities: Wilkinson, Gadalla (*Historical Deception, Egyptian Harmony, Egyptian Cosmology*), Hickmann (*Orientalische Musik, Musikgeschichte in Bildern: Ägypten*)

The Musical Pilgrimage: Gadalla (Egyptian Divinities)

Public Activities: Hickmann (*Orientalische Musik, Musikgeschichte in Bildern: Ägypten*), Wilkinson, Gadalla (*Egyptian Cosmology*)

21. Harmonic Sound Man

The Earthly Voyage: Blackman, Lane, Gadalla being a native Egyptian, Egyptian literature in Arabic

Sound Healing: Gadalla (*Egyptian Cosmology*)

Death and Resurrection: Sachs, Wilkinson, Gadalla (*Egyptian Cosmology*), Lane, Blackman

Gadalla as a native Egyptian

22. And The Beat Goes On

Herodotus, Plato, Blackman, Gadalla as a native Egyptian

Appendix A:- Western Musical Tampering

Sachs (*Our Musical Heritage*)

Appendix B: The Noise Makers

Sachs (*Wellsprings, Musicology*), and practically all other references

Appendix C: Pan Grecian Deceit

Gadalla (*Egyptian Cosmology*), Farmer (all his books, esp. *Sources of Arabian Music*)

Appendix D: Pre-Islamic Asiatic Neighbors

Sumer: Sachs (*History of Musical Instruments*)
The Assyrians: Engel, Stanford/Forsyth
The Persians: Engel, Gadalla (*Exiled Egyptians*)
The Hebrews: Sachs (*History of Musical Instruments* [Pentateuch]), Sachs (*Musicology*), Gadalla (*Historical Deception* [identity of David and Solomon]), Vantoura, Engel

Appendix E: Post-Islam Arabized/Islamized World

Gadalla (as a native Egyptian and born-Moslem), Farmer (*Historical Facts*), Touma

Index

C

D

E

F

G

H

I

J

K

L

M

N

O

S

T

U

V

W

X

Z

Tehuti Research Foundation

Tehuti Research Foundation (T.R.F.) is a non-profit, international organization, dedicated to Ancient Egyptian studies. Our books are engaging, factual, well researched, practical, interesting, and appealing to the general public. Visit our website at:

http://www.egypt-tehuti.org

E-mail address: info@egypt-tehuti.org

The books listed below are authored by T.R.F. chairman, Moustafa Gadalla.

Egyptian Cosmology: The Animated Universe - 2nd ed.

ISBN: 0-9652509-3-8 (pbk.), 192 pages, US$11.95

Egyptian cosmology is the ONLY metaphysics of all (ancient and modern) that is coherent, comprehensive, consistent, logical, analytical, and rational. The book surveys the applicability of Egyptian concepts to our modern understanding of the nature of the universe, creation, science, and philosophy. Discover the Egyptian concept of monotheism, number mysticism, the universal energy matrix, how the social and political structures were a reflection of the universe, and the interactions between the nine universal realms, ...etc.

Egyptian Divinities: The All Who Are THE ONE

ISBN: 1-931446-04-0 (pbk.), 128 pages, US$ 8.95

The Egyptian concept of God is based on recognizing the multiple attributes (gods/goddesses) of the Divine. Far from being a primitive, polytheistic concept, the Egyptian Way is the highest expression of monotheistic mysticism. The book details more than 80 divinities (gods/goddesses), how they act and interact to maintain the universe, and how they operate in the human being.

Egyptian Harmony: The Visual Music

ISBN: 0-9652509-8-9 (pbk.), 192 pages, US$11.95

This book reveals the Ancient Egyptian incredible and comprehensive knowledge of harmonic proportion, sacred geometry, and number mysticism, as manifested in their texts, temples, tombs, ...etc., throughout their known history. Discover how the Word (sound) that created the World (forms) was likewise transformed to visual music by the Egyptians into hieroglyphs, art, and architecture. The book surveys the Ancient Egyptian harmonic proportional application in all aspects of their civilization.

Historical Deception
The Untold Story of Ancient Egypt - 2nd Edition

ISBN: 0-9652509-2-X (pbk.), 352 pages, US$19.95

This book reveals the ingrained prejudices against Ancient Egypt, from religious groups, who deny that Egypt is the source of their creed, and Western academicians, who deny the existence of science and philosophy prior to the Greeks. The book contains 46 chapters, with many interesting topics, such as the Egyptian medical knowledge about determining the sex of the unborn, and much, much more.

Exiled Egyptians: The Heart of Africa

ISBN: 0-9652509-6-2 (pbk.), 352 pages, US$19.95

Read about the forgotten Ancient Egyptians, who fled the foreign invasions and religious oppressions, and rebuilt the Ancient Egyptian model system in Africa, when Egypt itself became an Arab colony. Find out how a thousand years of Islamic jihads have fragmented and dispersed the African continent into endless misery and chaos. Discover the true causes and dynamics of the history of African slavery. Understand the genius of the Ancient Egyptian/African religious, social, economical, and political systems.

Pyramid Handbook - Second Edition

ISBN: 0-9652509-4-6 (pbk.), 192 pages, US$11.95

A complete handbook about the pyramids of Ancient Egypt during the Pyramid Age. It contains: the locations and dimensions of interiors and exteriors of the pyramids; the history and builders of the pyramids; theories of construction; theories on their purpose and function; the sacred geometry that was incorporated into the design of the pyramids; and much, much more.

Tut-Ankh-Amen: The Living Image of the Lord

ISBN: 0-9652509-9-7 (pbk.), 144 pages, US$9.50

This book provides the overwhelming evidence from archeology, the Dead Sea Scrolls, the Talmud, and the Bible itself, that Tut-Ankh-Amen was the historical character of Jesus. The book examines the details of Tut's birth, life, death, resurrection, family roots, religion, teachings, etc., which were duplicated in the biblical account of Jesus.

Egypt: A Practical Guide

ISBN: 0-9652509-3-0 (pbk.), 256 pages, US$8.50

A no-nonsense, no-clutter, practical guide to Egypt, written by an Egyptian-American Egyptologist. Quick, easy, and comprehensive reference to sites of antiquities and recreation. Find your way with numerous maps and illustrations.

Egyptian Sufism: The Hidden Treasure

ISBN: 1-931446-05-9 (pbk.), 192 pages, US$11.95

Discover the Ancient Egyptian roots of Sufism and its affiliates: gnosticism, alchemy, freemasonry, ...etc. Pursue the treasure within, for Sufism is in (and for) everyone. Find out the correlation between the Ancient Egyptian Sufi calendar of events and the heavenly movements of the planets.

Tehuti Research Foundation

Ordering Information

Name ____

Address ____

City ____

State/Province _______________________________________

Country __________________Tel. (_____) _____________

______ *books* @ $14.95 (*Egyptian Rhythm*) = $

______ *books* @ $11.95 (*Egyptian Cosmology*) = $

______ *books* @ $ 8.95 (*Egyptian Divinities*) = $

______ *books* @ $11.95 (*Egyptian Harmony*) = $

______ *books* @ $19.95 (*Historical Deception*) = $

______ *books* @ $19.95 (*Exiled Egyptians*) = $

______ *books* @ $11.95 (*Pyramid Handbook*) = $

______ *books* @ $ 9.50 (*Tut-Ankh-Amen*) = $

______ *books* @ $ 8.50 (*Egypt: Pract. Guide*) = $

______ *books* @ $11.95 (*Egyptian Sufism*) = $________

Subtotal = $

North Carolina residents, add 6 % Sales Tax = $

Shipping: (U.S.A. only) $2.00 for 1st book = $

for each additional book $1 x _____ = $

Outside U.S.A. (per weight/destination) = $________

Total = $

Payment: [ ] Check (payable: Tehuti Research Foundation)

[ ] Visa [ ] MasterCard [ ] Discover

Card Number: ____

Name on Card: _______________________ Exp. Date: ___/___

Tehuti Research Foundation

P.O. Box 39406

Greensboro, NC 27438-9406 U.S.A.

Call TOLL FREE (North America) and order now 888-826-7021

Or FAX your order 212-656-1460

e-mail: info@egypt-tehuti.org